NICK GRAY *with* LAURA SCANDIFFIO

A True Story

ESCAPE from TIBET

FOREWORD BY

HIS HOLINESS THE DALAI LAMA

annick press
toronto + new york + vancouver

We acknowledge the support of the Canada Council for the Arts, the Ontario Arts
Council, and the Government of Canada through the Canada Book Fund (CBF)
for our publishing activities.

Cataloging in Publication
Gray, Nick, author
    Escape from Tibet : a true story / Nick Gray ; with Laura Scandiffio.

Issued in print and electronic formats.
ISBN 978-1-55451-663-6 (bound).–ISBN 978-1-55451-662-9 (pbk.).–
ISBN 978-1-55451-665-0 (pdf).–ISBN 978-1-55451-664-3 (epub)

    1. Tibet Autonomous Region (China)–History–1951- –Juvenile
literature. 2. Tibet Autonomous Region (China)–Biography–Juvenile
literature. 3. Tibetans–Great Britain–Biography–Juvenile literature.
I. Scandiffio, Laura, author II. Title.

DS786.G67 2014   951'.5050922   C2014-901948-3
                                            C2014-901949-1

Distributed in Canada by: Published in the U.S.A. by:
Firefly Books Ltd.   Annick Press (U.S.) Ltd.
50 Staples Avenue, Unit 1   Distributed in the U.S.A. by:
Richmond Hill, ON   Firefly Books (U.S.) Inc.
L4B 1H1   P.O. Box 1338, Ellicott Station
                                   Buffalo, NY 14205

Printed in Canada

Visit us at: www.annickpress.com
Visit Nick Gray at: www.escapefromtibet.org
Visit Laura Scandiffio at: www.laurascandiffio.com

Also available in e-book format. Please visit www.annickpress.com/ebooks.html
for more details. Or scan

MIX
Paper from
responsible sources
FSC® C004071

This book is dedicated
to the thousands of
Tibetans who have chosen
exile from their homeland
by climbing over
the Himalayas.

➤

THE DALAI LAMA

FOREWORD

It is now more than fifty years since events in my homeland compelled me and many tens of thousands of other Tibetans to seek asylum in India. We not only lost our freedom, but the very survival of our culture and our identity as a people is continually undermined.

I believe it is important for the international community to speak up on behalf of the Tibetan people, because the survival of Tibet's Buddhist culture concerns not only six million Tibetans, but also millions of people in the Himalayan and Mongolian regions who regard it with respect. Being based on the principles of nonviolence and compassion Tibetan culture has the potential to contribute to a more peaceful and harmonious world.

What happens in Tibet also affects the fragile environment of Tibet and the entire Himalayan region, which in turn has an impact on the the lives of billions of people across South and South-east Asia. In addition, a meaningful solution of the Tibetan issue will contribute to peace and security in the wider vicinity of Tibet that is home to more than a third of the world's population.

Today Tibet is passing through a very critical period; the Chinese government's unremitting efforts to assimilate Tibetans is eroding the Tibetan people's distinct cultural and spiritual heritage. Such material improvements as have been made in life in Tibet have not brought the contentment that might have been expected; life for Tibetans in Tibet remains very difficult.

Even today Tibetans continue to make the difficult and dangerous journey across the Himalayas in search of the education and freedom to live as Tibetans that they are denied in their homeland. This story of two brothers escaping from Tibet and the hardships they endured describes the common experience of many Tibetans who over the years like them fled into exile.

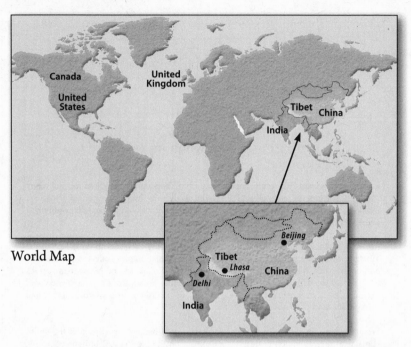

World Map

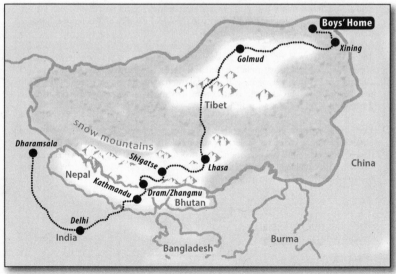

Pasang and Tenzin's route from their home in northeast Tibet
to Dharamsala, in India

INTRODUCTION

The aim of this book is to shine a light on what is, for many, a dark corner of the world. The brothers Tenzin and Pasang were born and raised in northeastern Tibet, in the center of Asia, far from Europe and North America, far even from the sea, high up on the Tibetan plateau. They are members of an oppressed people. The Chinese Communist government has ruled their country since the 1950s. This book tells the story of the brothers' escape from their point of view—to describe their struggle for freedom from a personal perspective. Their unique experience offers a rare opportunity to better understand the many dangers that refugees from Tibet face in their quest for freedom.

Tenzin's escape from Tibet with his elder brother Pasang seems an unbelievable story of horror and heroism. But it is true. Nick Gray first met the brothers while making a documentary film exposing the plight of the Tibetan people, and has remained friends with them ever since. He was a witness to some of their journey, and has visited many of the places where the events of their story took place, including the

1

brothers' home in Tibet. In the last few years, the brothers have shared with him extensive descriptions of their experiences and feelings during their escape, and this book is a faithful record of their accounts. However, their names and those of their fellow escapers have been changed.

Only now are the brothers willing to have the full story of their escape from Tibet told, an authentic record of what refugees, including children, will attempt in order to achieve freedom from oppression.

Nick Gray and Laura Scandiffio

PROLOGUE

Return of the Fugitive

In the clear, moonlit night, a shadowy figure leaned against the courtyard wall, while those inside the house slept, unaware of its presence. Outlined against the sky was the dark shape of a man, tall and thin, his shoulders stooped with exhaustion. He had walked fifty miles from the nearest town, and had reached this tiny village, which clung to a Tibetan hillside, with only the moon's pale light to guide him. But he was no stranger. For him it was the end of a long, long journey. He had left this place as a thirteen-year-old boy, a novice monk. Now he returned as a young eighteen-year-old man.

He was so weary that for a time he rested against the familiar metal door to the courtyard. On either side stretched the high, thick mud walls that kept the yard cool in summer and warm in winter. But the well-known surroundings only awoke painful memories. Those awful days after his father died came back, vivid in his mind. "You must grow up quickly now," his mother had told him.

3

He shut his eyes for an instant, as if to block the flood of memory. For a few moments longer he lingered in the doorway, uncertain. He listened, but could hear no sound from the house. Even the animals were fast asleep. He pictured his three brothers sleeping inside—Dorje, Tenzin, and young Palden. He longed to talk to them. They would be older now, different from the memories he had carried with him. His body remained still, but his mind was in turmoil. How would his mother and brothers react when they saw him? For five years there had been no contact, not since he had run away from the monastery where his mother had sent him. He imagined how frantic she must have been at first, then mournful, and perhaps, finally, giving up hope. What would she say to him now? He straightened up and took a deep breath.

The metal door was locked, but he expected that at night. He paced around the outer walls, looking for another way into the courtyard. Finally, at one corner he found a foothold and clambered up.

"Open the door!" he called over the wall, his hoarse voice shattering the silence. "Open the door—" He almost added "Mother," but it had been so long since he had used that word, it caught in his throat.

Inside, the house dog barked. The bark turned to a whimper. Had he recognized the voice calling outside? The young man felt tears sting his eyes as he clung to the wall top. He called again.

"Who is it?" From somewhere inside, his mother's familiar voice quavered. She sounded frightened. "Leave us alone."

"It's me, Pasang!" he cried out.

But she didn't believe him. He called out his name many times before she opened the door, just wide enough to peek through. Pasang darted for the doorway, but his mother caught him by the wrists. Her grip was strong. As she blocked his way, moonlight fell across his face. She relaxed her hold and stared up at him.

"Have the gods dropped you from the sky? My son, have you come back to me?" She began to sob.

This was too much for Pasang. Overcome, he dropped to his knees. She knelt next to him, and they held each other, weeping. For the first time in many years, they were tears of pure joy.

Yet even as he felt his mother's arms enfold him, Pasang was already wondering how he would tell her. How would he explain that this was no simple homecoming? He hadn't returned just to stay and go back to their old ways. He had come here with a purpose, a plan she would certainly call reckless. Yes, he knew, she would resist it. But he had to find a way, somehow, to convince her.

CHAPTER 1

Strangers in Their Own Country

Before dawn, Tenzin woke from restless dreams. He lay quietly for a moment, trying to recall them. He remembered hearing the dog bark, and voices. Or had that been part of his dreams? There were voices even now, close by. He opened his eyes and looked around the small room where his family ate and slept. The central stove was already lit. Next to it, he was startled to see his mother talking to a tall man, his back to Tenzin. He wore the long robes of a Buddhist monk. The stranger abruptly turned. He ran his hand through his thick black hair, and smiled at Tenzin, lines creasing around weary eyes. It was a young man's face—gaunt and weather-beaten, but young—and the eyes were kind. There was something familiar about them. Tenzin blinked, uncertain. His mother laughed.

"See, it's Pasang. He's been to India and back!"

"Pasang!" Tenzin leapt from his bed and threw his arms around his older brother. Looking up at him, he was astonished by how tall Pasang was, how strong he seemed now. Eight years older than ten-year-old Tenzin, the person smiling down at him was no longer the boy who had left home to become a monk. He was a man. Tenzin stepped back, suddenly shy.

"He came home last night," his mother explained. "He kept calling for me to let him in, but at first I didn't believe it was him! I thought some troublemaker was playing a cruel joke." Her words came fast, bubbling like a stream. "Then I saw his face," she added, and broke off. Tenzin stared at her. He couldn't remember when he'd last seen her looking so happy.

"I thought I'd get the scolding of a lifetime," Pasang said, smiling slyly.

Tenzin glanced at his mother, but she was shaking her head, gazing at Pasang. Tenzin wondered if Pasang realized just how much their mother had worried. He had vanished from the monastery, without a word. Police had come to the house to warn them that Pasang was in deep trouble: Chinese laws decreed that all Tibetans must stay where they were registered. No one could travel to another province without permission; leaving the country was strictly forbidden. Often Tenzin had woken in the night to hear the drone of his mother's voice, praying for Pasang. Tenzin used to picture him, wandering somewhere alone in the world. It was hard for him to imagine; Tenzin had left their village just once in his life, and that was only to go to Pasang's monastery. Thinking of Pasang so far away had made him shiver with a strange fear. But it was a fear mixed with admiration. Imagine being so brave!

By now everyone was awake, and Tenzin's brothers Palden and Dorje pushed past him to greet Pasang. They settled at last on Tenzin's bed, and Pasang handed out gifts. A watermelon, sunflower seeds—treats rarely seen in their village. Tenzin munched on the fried seeds as Pasang began to pass around photographs. Tenzin gazed at the pictures of unfamiliar young men in monks' robes—Pasang's friends from a monastery, far away in India. Tenzin had no idea how far that was, but he knew it was beyond the Snow Mountains.

Carefully, Pasang retrieved one last picture from the folds of his robe and held it up: it was a laminated photo of a man, dressed like a monk, wearing glasses. Tenzin gazed at the face, round like his own; it had a friendly, open expression.

"I saw him," Pasang said, his voice nearly a whisper. "He came to the temple of our monastery in India."

Tenzin realized at once who it was. There was a name that no one was allowed to speak, in case the Chinese police might hear. Sometimes Tenzin said it silently to himself in his head: *Dalai Lama.* It was the name of the spiritual leader of the Tibetan people. Tenzin also knew that secretly, beneath her bed, his mother kept a picture of this man with the forbidden name. Sometimes, to receive the holy man's blessing, she raised the photograph to touch her forehead, before pressing it onto Tenzin's, and murmuring a prayer.

Tenzin knew very little about the Dalai Lama, except that he no longer lived in Tibet, but in India. Where Pasang had gone! He leaned in for a closer look at the monk with spectacles and a kindly smile.

His mother gently took the image from Pasang and touched it to the top of her head. Wordlessly, she passed it back to Pasang, who tucked it back under his robe. He sighed, and suddenly his shoulders drooped. She reached for his hand.

"You're so tired. Look, you can hardly stay awake. We will hear all about your adventures when you have rested."

Tenzin nearly burst with impatience. "But I want to know everything!" he blurted out. "Where have you been all this time? What have you been doing?"

"Yes, of course," said Pasang, smiling wearily, "I'll tell you everything. There's a lot to tell, but later. Now I need some sleep, maybe for a hundred years."

"And you," his mother said, turning to Tenzin, "need to go to school."

"But not today! Not with Pasang back—"

"Yes, today," his mother said sternly. "Pasang needs to rest."

Tenzin groaned. At least, he thought, he'd have something exciting to tell his cousin. "Wait until Sangye hears—"

Pasang's eyes flashed. "Don't say a word about me, not to Sangye, not to anyone, do you hear?" Tenzin flinched at the sudden fierceness in his voice.

Then Pasang sighed and his expression softened. "If the police find out I'm here, they'll arrest me and . . ." He glanced at their mother, whose brow was knotted with worry. "We'd all be in trouble. So not a word, okay?"

Tenzin nodded. He had nearly forgotten how quickly Pasang used to lose his temper. Feeling shy again, he eyed this new, older Pasang with a feeling of awe. Well, he wouldn't let his brother down; he'd stay quiet. But it wasn't going to be easy. Going to school today was bad enough, but keeping his secret all day long, that was going to be agony.

➤

Tenzin picked up his pace as he trotted downhill toward the center of the village. He was late, and the last thing he wanted today was to draw attention to himself by getting in trouble. Joining the other stragglers headed for the school courtyard, he glanced up at the plain brick-and-cement building with distaste.

Even though he was nearly eleven, Tenzin had gone to school for only the past three years—and was far from used to it. Behind barred windows, the Chinese teachers drilled sixty students on China's history and language. Tenzin often struggled to look alert through yet another lecture by Mr. Head Teacher Yang on "Heroes of World Communism." Tenzin knew very well that the Chinese were not his people; they were the invaders of his country. His mother wanted him to learn Tibet's language and history, and study their Buddhist religion, but the Chinese authorities forbade it. And so Tenzin spoke very little Tibetan, since everyone in his village used the local northern dialect, and he heard only Chinese at school.

"They make me feel like a stranger in my own country," Tenzin often heard her say.

As students streamed through the front gate for morning assembly, Tenzin fell into step with Sangye.

"Hey, Tenzin!" Sangye grinned. "You're huffing and puffing. You look as red as your scarf!"

"Speak in Chinese, Sangye." Tenzin nudged his friend. "Mister Yang might hear us."

Standing in their ranks in the courtyard, the students gave a plausible impression of unity—all wearing the uniform of white shirt, dark blue trousers, and regulation red scarf, a symbol of the Communist Party. Together they sang the Chinese national anthem, while a senior boy hoisted the Chinese flag up the central pole. Mister Yang, flanked by five other teachers, watched the rows of students closely. In his right hand he held a short stick. Tenzin winced as he glanced at it: he knew how much pain that stick could inflict.

Inside the classroom, Tenzin's teacher stood frowning under the sign that proclaimed *Love the Nation and Obey the Laws.* Like a stern commander surveying unsatisfactory troops, he watched his students for signs of inattention. Tenzin understood little of what his teacher shouted in Chinese. But he had learned to look as if he did. He knew he would be in for a harsh punishment if the teacher suspected he wasn't listening. He'd watched his classmates get smacked with the stick or kicked in the legs—one teacher had even hit a boy over the head with a chair. Many times Tenzin had gone home bruised and sore.

The morning dragged by. When the school gong sounded for the lunch break, Tenzin felt like a prisoner set free. He slid off his classroom stool and quickly found Sangye. Together they made a run for it through the school gates. It was risky, but Tenzin was sure none of the teachers had noticed. They raced each other to the river, their bottles of salted black tea banging against their legs. Tenzin was shorter and sturdier than his cousin, but faster than he looked. He outran him easily, savoring the feeling of freedom. At the riverbank he skidded to a halt, Sangye at his heels.

"How come you were late this morning?" Sangye quizzed him.

Tenzin shrugged. "I slept in," he muttered. He had an uncomfortable feeling; usually he told Sangye everything. He felt his cousin staring at him. Avoiding Sangye's eyes, he changed the subject, pointing to some rocks in the shallows of the river.

"That's where I saw the really big one." The excitement of Pasang's return made him feel impulsive, almost reckless. "I'm going in!" he added.

Sangye laughed as he watched Tenzin pull off his shoes and wade into the water. Soon he was up to his knees in the current, bare toes clinging to the pebbles. There he stood, as still as he could, watching. He gasped and lunged as a silvery fish swam by. And another. And another. He missed them all.

"You'll never catch anything!" Sangye taunted him.

Tenzin plunged forward again. This time his fingers closed around a fish's slippery underside.

"I've got one!" he cried, triumphant. "Look!" He could hardly believe it.

He hurled the fish toward Sangye on the bank, and waded out. The plump fish lay on the ground, its eye glittering, gills pumping hard. The two boys stared down at it, and then at each other.

"What do we do now?" asked Tenzin.

"Eat it!" Sangye snickered. "You can eat them, you know. I've seen it at a festival. They fry them and eat them hot, with pepper sauce."

Tenzin had never heard of anyone eating a fish before. Suddenly he felt very keenly how few things he had seen, how few places he had been. But he wasn't going to show Sangye how little he knew.

"I don't believe you!" He crossed his arms and frowned. "They're so . . . slimy . . . and smelly." They looked at each other, and burst out laughing.

"I know what to do," said Tenzin finally. "Let's put it back."

He picked up the fish and, crouching down by the water's edge, gently let it wriggle free through his fingers. They watched it swim away.

The boys sat down to drink their tea. Tenzin dug out the bread and biscuits his mother had packed in his bag and ate hungrily. He was glad Sangye was too busy eating to ask him any more questions. Wiping his forearm across his mouth, Tenzin slumped onto the grass, closing his eyes against the glare of the sun. The bright green of the hillside in spring was almost too brilliant to look at. Since the snows had melted, everything was growing fast. He thought of how, in a few weeks, he would be working long days helping his mother weed the fields of crops. At the top of the valley lay the grazing pastures for sheep, and ever since he could walk, Tenzin had taken his turn on the high hills as a shepherd. But now that Pasang was back, everything would be different, better.

"If you think fish are weird, you should see the freak show at the festival," Sangye said, breaking the silence. "I saw a creature with a baby's body and a monkey's head."

"Really?" Tenzin opened one eye and wrinkled his nose in disbelief.

"Yeah, it was pickled in a bottle. There was a human head with a snake's body, too. And a two-headed baby!"

"Sangye, you talk a lot of nonsense."

"How would you know? You've never seen a freak show. Anyway, I saw them with my own eyes." After a moment, Sangye sighed. "I guess they can't be real, though, can they?"

His eyes glinted. "But you know, you're a bit of a freak. I'd pay to see you pickled in a bottle!"

"Hey!" Tenzin cried. He lunged at his friend, with half a mind to tip him into the river. But Sangye had already jumped up.

"Come on, let's go."

Tenzin pushed himself up to his feet. "All right! Keep up, then!" he shouted over his shoulder as he darted back up to the road.

➤

After school, Tenzin and Sangye walked home together, stepping off the road as a truck full of Chinese troops roared by. The soldiers seemed to be everywhere—by the school, in the village, on the road along the river. But now the sight of them in their helmets and camouflage uniforms made Tenzin's heart beat faster, as he thought of Pasang hidden at home. They waited until the truck had passed, leaving behind a cloud of dust.

Outside Sangye's house Tenzin gave his friend a quick wave good-bye, and continued up the rocky track to his own home farther uphill. He was exhausted and hungry. It was the same every day. He never seemed to have enough to eat.

He thought of how his father had once farmed the land higher up the valley, where he grew barley and beans. The family had kept a donkey, some cows, pigs, and a woolly yak, too. There must have been good food then, but Tenzin could hardly remember it. When Tenzin was still very young, his father had become terribly sick.

His mother had sold everything she could—livestock and land—to pay for his hospital treatment. But the medicine did little good, and his father died. Tenzin could remember his mother calling them into the room where he lay and seeing his dead body. She told them to pray for him. But that was all he could recall.

Once Pasang had left, Tenzin lived with his mother and two brothers: Dorje, who was older, and little Palden, born shortly before their father died. He would be starting school in a few months.

Dorje had gone to the same school as Tenzin, until one day a teacher punished him with blows to the head. To everyone's shock, Dorje hit the teacher back. He was expelled from school, and the family was publicly humiliated. It wasn't Dorje's fault, Tenzin knew; he was a bit slow. His mother had once told Tenzin that when Dorje was little, she'd thought that he was deaf and dumb. She went to the village wise man, who told her to take her son to the monastery. If he licked the door handle, he would be cured. Shortly after that Dorje found his voice, but he always spoke slowly. Tenzin knew that he was better at farm work than thinking.

Tenzin picked up his pace as he neared home. His excitement was making him forget his hunger. *Pasang will be awake by now,* he thought. He'd ask him about India and everywhere he'd been. In his hurry, he barely noticed the unfamiliar motorbike leaning against the courtyard wall. Eagerly he pushed open the backyard gate, ringing the brass bell. Rushing through, he nearly collided with a stocky man in uniform.

"Where is your brother Pasang?" a stern voice demanded.

Two Chinese police officers stood in the courtyard, barring Tenzin's way. He stared at them in horror. How had they found out about Pasang so soon? Before he could think of an answer, one of the men grabbed his arm and shook him. Tenzin cried out—the grip on his arm hurt like a vice.

"Where is he? We know he is here!"

Tenzin's mind raced. What if they barged their way in—how could he hide Pasang? But at that moment his brother stepped out into the yard. He stood squarely before the two men. The officer dropped Tenzin's arm.

"You're Pasang, eh?" he sneered accusingly. "Why have you come back? Isn't India good enough for you?" Pasang said nothing and avoided the officer's eyes. This seemed to enrage the man even more. He turned red in the face as he glared at Pasang.

"We're watching you this time," he bellowed. "If you try to escape again, you will be caught, and thrown into prison. And we will confiscate everything." He looked around, waving his arms at the house and compound.

Tenzin bit his lip. He knew families had been thrown out of their homes and off their land. These men could easily make that happen—or they could take Pasang away at any moment.

The second officer stepped forward and jabbed a finger at Pasang's face. "You must report to the local police station. We have documents for you to sign, and you will be fingerprinted. We have our eyes on you. You are not to leave the area without official permission—which will *not* be granted."

Tenzin watched Pasang closely. He continued to stand passively, but now he was red with anger. Tenzin could still remember how much Pasang hated being told what to do. He cringed, waiting for the outburst. Pasang would shout; the men would seize him, drag him away . . .

But nothing happened.

The officers turned and pushed their way through the metal gate. Tenzin listened to the sound of their motorbike roaring to life, the engine's drone eventually fading in the distance. Pasang stood glowering after them, breathing hard. The hatred in his face almost frightened Tenzin. When he spoke at last, it was like a hiss under his breath.

"They will not tie me up like a dog."

He turned without looking at Tenzin and went into the house. Tenzin followed closely, suddenly afraid to lose sight of him. His happy mood was shattered. In its place, a fear began to gnaw inside him. Despite the officers' threats, something told him his brother wouldn't stay for long now.

After their chores were done, it was dark by the time the family sat down to share a meal of pork, noodles, and boiled greens. More food than usual, in honor of Pasang's return. Tenzin filled his bowl and ate greedily.

Pasang ate without speaking. No one mentioned the police visit.

"Have you ever eaten a fish, mother?" Tenzin asked, to break the silence.

His mother frowned. "We don't eat fish. Anyway, they look like a mass of smelly bones. Meat is best."

Tenzin stared at his empty bowl, his stomach still not satisfied.

His mother whisked away the empty dishes. "Now you two are going to bed," she commanded abruptly, nodding at Tenzin and Palden. She shortened the wick in the oil lamp.

Tenzin sighed. Bedtime was always early now, to save oil. There would be no stories of India and adventures tonight.

➤

Tenzin stayed watchful, but as spring turned to summer, Pasang did not disappear as he had dreaded. All through the warm months Tenzin kept busy, but whether he was herding sheep or searching for wild honey, his mind was never completely at ease. He shuddered each time he sighted the police stalking through the village. He knew they hounded Pasang, often stopping him and demanding to see his papers.

Fall came and Tenzin went back to school, working every evening and weekend alongside his mother and Dorje in the fields. Pasang was restricted by the police to his old monastery, where he once again took up his training to be a monk. The police had threatened him with reprisals against his family if he even talked about leaving the area. Pasang clearly despised them.

"They won't arrest me—not yet. They like to keep us under their thumb," he told Tenzin with disgust. "If we had any money, they'd demand a bribe. As it is, mother's had to give them potatoes. They were annoyed we had no meat."

Pasang's monastery did, however, allow him some visits home. And as the monastery was in the same county as the village, the police did not interfere. Tenzin waited impatiently for him each time.

"Tell me what happened next!" he blurted out one evening as Pasang walked through the door. Tenzin could not hear enough of his brother's adventures.

Pasang laughed. "To get to India I climbed over the Snow Mountains—the highest place in the world," he said, taking his usual spot near the stove.

Tenzin listened, eyes wide, drinking in every word. He tried to picture those thousands of miles, the mountains reaching up to the heavens, but he had never been farther than Pasang's monastery. It seemed impossible—exciting but terribly frightening. How had Pasang done it? But Pasang didn't talk for long of his travels; he never did. His answers to Tenzin's questions became vague, as if hinting that more had happened than he could ever tell. Then Pasang's eyes grew distant, and he changed the subject. Tenzin knew he would have to wait for his next glimpse of that faraway world.

The months went by and snow covered the hills. Tenzin looked forward to the start of the Tibetan New Year in February. With Pasang home, it would be different. For the first time in so many years, they would celebrate it together.

On the day the festival began, like all the other families, the four brothers and their mother walked up to the cemetery at the top of the village to pray at the graves of their ancestors. Standing at their father's graveside, Tenzin shivered in the cold. He shuffled from one foot to the other, unsure what to pray for. He raised his eyes to sneak a glance at his mother. This year her face didn't look sad. Her gaze lingered on each of her four sons, a mixture of tenderness and pride in her eyes.

Back home they all helped to prepare the traditional New Year's feast. In all the bustle, Tenzin felt a new optimism. The Year of the Dog was about to begin; it would be the year of "loyalty and caring with a fearless streak." *That must mean good things are in store for all of us,* Tenzin thought.

Yet in the days that followed, Tenzin noticed a change in his mother. There was something anxious in her expression, and when he talked to her she seemed distracted. Something wasn't right, but he couldn't work out what it was. More than once he heard Pasang speaking quietly but urgently to her, while she kept her face turned away from him. When they spotted Tenzin nearby, Pasang would stop, then begin talking loudly about something ordinary. Tenzin wasn't fooled. Something was wrong, and no one was telling him anything.

A strange tension hung in the air, like storm clouds overhead. When he noticed his mother watching Pasang, he knew she sensed it too. But as usual, she didn't share what she was thinking with Tenzin. The fear that had gripped him when the police came returned now. Pasang meant more to Tenzin than he could ever explain. He was like an older brother and father at the same time.

Very soon, Tenzin thought, *I'm going to lose him again.*

CHAPTER 2

A Great Journey

"**C**ome on, *get in.*"

Pasang sounded a little impatient this time. Tenzin stared up at his brother where he sat in the family's donkey cart, holding the reins, his monk's red robes draped around him. Next to him sat their mother, tense and still. Tenzin looked questioningly at her, but she turned away.

Tenzin hesitated a little longer, then climbed over the side. It didn't make sense. He always walked to school. Why did Pasang want to take him in the cart all of a sudden?

"*Durr! Durr!*" Pasang shouted at the donkey. "Move!" Reluctantly, the old animal jerked forward. The cart rattled out of the courtyard, and Tenzin looked back. Dorje and Palden stood in the doorway, staring at them. Tenzin faced ahead, clutching the bag of bread, biscuits, and tea he always took to school. No one spoke. By the way his mother's shoulders shook, he could tell she was crying.

At the bottom of the hill the cart splashed through the stream where they collected their water. Pasang tightened the reins and the cart turned sharply. This was not the way to school. Tenzin couldn't stand it any longer.

He tugged on Pasang's arm. "What's happening, Pasang?" He found himself whispering, without knowing why. "Have I done something wrong?"

Pasang looked down at him, then turned to their mother. "Are you going to tell him, or shall I?"

She merely nodded. Tenzin's heart was pounding now. Pasang shook the reins and paused before he spoke.

"You're not going to school today," he said at last. "You're going away with me, on a great journey—past the Snow Mountains, to India."

Tenzin blinked. "What?" was all he could gasp.

"We couldn't tell you before," Pasang went on. "You might have told your friends at school and the police would have been on to us in no time. And this way, no one in our family will be branded a 'traitor to the Motherland.'" His mouth twisted in derision at these last words. "We leave suddenly—and mother and the rest can say they knew nothing of it."

He turned to look at Tenzin. The angry light in his eyes was gone now and he smiled. "Don't look so worried," he said, nudging him. "We're going on an adventure."

Tenzin stared at the dirt road ahead. His head was reeling. They passed the familiar hills, green with spring grass. But everything was different now. The fresh air, the patches of wildflowers, even the flies buzzing around the donkey's head seemed more vivid, filling his senses. Slowly Pasang's words began to sink in. A wave of excitement took hold of him. Could it really be true?

"But when did you decide all this?" Tenzin wondered aloud.

"I told Mother that it's the only way," Pasang answered firmly. "She's working herself to death, scrounging enough food from what's left of our farm, and still there's not enough to eat. I said it was time *I* did something for this family. I know she needs Dorje to help her, so I said I would take Palden with me and look after him. We'd have a good life in another place—free from the police—where we could do more with our lives than just survive, and one day we would come back. 'Palden is too young,' she told me."

Pasang turned to face Tenzin.

"So I am taking you," he finished simply.

The cart pulled up near the village bus stop. Tenzin clambered down. It all seemed dreamlike, strange but thrilling. He felt giddy, almost ready to laugh, but when he looked at his mother's serious face, he stopped himself.

As they waited for the bus, Tenzin spotted Sangye across the road. He was with some other boys from school. Tenzin opened his mouth to call, but Pasang grabbed his arm.

"Quiet! Stand behind me."

Tenzin slunk guiltily behind his brother. He would have to be more careful than that! Pasang was counting on him, and he must not disappoint him. Peeking around his brother's back, he glimpsed his friends disappearing around a corner.

Moments later Tenzin recognized the sound of the bus climbing the hill, its gears grinding on the steep ascent. Pasang heard it too. He turned to their mother.

"Remember, if the police come for us, tell them we're visiting cousins in Lhasa. That's all you know." His voice was a hoarse whisper.

The bus appeared over the crest of the hill, its brakes hissing as it halted before them. Their mother thrust some money into Pasang's hands, then hugged him. She turned to Tenzin next and took him in her arms. Her embrace was so tight it hurt, but Tenzin didn't want her to let go.

"Look after yourselves. Come back soon. Never forget me," she said, then released him.

Tenzin's dreamy excitement fell away. Suddenly this was all terribly real.

He followed his brother up the bus steps and took his seat next to him in silence. His heart beat fast as the bus pulled away, scattering stones. Tenzin looked back through the window. He could see his mother throwing wheat grains in the air: an offering to the gods to protect travelers from evil. Tenzin kept his eyes on her until the bus's exhaust fumes hid her, and she disappeared from view. She was gone.

Tenzin turned around and leaned closer to Pasang's shoulder. He had never been away from his mother for more than a few hours. The bus passed his school, and he thought of Sangye inside. Was it really possible he would never return there? He had no regrets about that. It was a place where he had always felt confused and hurt—stung by the teacher's stick, told he was inferior. But what about Sangye and the others? He could hardly imagine life without them.

Tenzin sat back and closed his eyes as the bus lurched along the dirt road. *When I see them again,* he told himself, *I'll have such stories to tell!*

His brother's voice startled him.

"Please, driver, stop the bus!" Pasang shouted. He jumped to his feet and ran down the aisle. Alarmed, Tenzin followed.

Pasang spoke rapidly to the driver, begging him to let them off. Tenzin tugged Pasang's robe.

"What is it?" he asked. "Are we going back?" Pasang didn't answer.

The bus came to a halt, and Pasang led Tenzin back down the steps. The driver sped off, leaving them in a trail of dust on the road.

Maybe Pasang had lost confidence in him. Had he spoiled everything somehow?

"Pasang, why did you change your mind?" Tenzin pleaded.

"I haven't," Pasang said, staring back toward the village. "I've remembered something. Something important." He knelt down and put his hands on Tenzin's shoulders. "I need you to stay here. I'll be back, and we'll catch the next bus, all right?"

Tenzin nodded, bewildered. What could be so important? His mind raced, but he wasn't going to show how alarmed he felt.

Pasang seemed to sense his confusion. "It'll be okay," he said gently. "Just stay out of sight. Hide in the trees, and wait for me. I'll be back soon."

He pushed his bundle of clothes into Tenzin's hands. Without another word he turned and ran up the road.

Tenzin watched him for a moment, blinking in the dust. Then he walked into the little wood alongside the road, and sat behind a tree. Butterflies flitted past as he listened to birdsong and the buzz of bees. There was no other sound. An age seemed to pass, and still no Pasang.

When his brother reappeared at last, breathless from running, Tenzin could have cried from relief.

"Don't worry, there's another bus coming," Pasang said, panting as he dropped down next to Tenzin. "But look at these. I nearly forgot them." He held out two red cords. Tenzin recognized them. They were blessing strings. Travelers wore them around their necks to guarantee the protection of the gods. Now he understood.

"Mother made them and gave them to me last night," Pasang explained. "I *had* to go back to get them. If I didn't, she would think that something terrible was going to happen to us. But now we'll have good luck."

Tenzin swallowed. "Did you see her?" he asked.

Pasang paused and looked down at the ground. "She was on her knees, with her face in her hands, making a terrible noise," he said quietly. "I couldn't face her, so I grabbed the strings and ran out. She never knew I'd been there."

He raised his eyes. Tenzin nodded. Wordlessly, he took his string from Pasang's hand and put it around his neck. Leaning back against the tree, he slowly tied the most complicated knot he knew, so he would never lose it.

➤

Pasang was right. It wasn't long before another bus picked them up. For two hours they traveled through small villages and fields of crops. The excitement of setting out faded, and Tenzin felt exhausted. The drone and swaying of the bus made his eyes heavy, and he dozed off.

"Wake up, Tenzin." Pasang was nudging him. "We're almost there."

Tenzin sat up and looked fearfully around. The bus was now crowded with passengers. Tenzin saw that he was by far the youngest on board. His anxiety grew. He felt as if everyone was watching him, wondering who he was and what he was doing so far from home.

Don't be stupid, he told himself. *They probably don't care. Sit still and no one will even notice you.*

Pasang had told him their journey would begin in Xining—a great, bustling city. Tenzin had never seen a city, great or small, in his life. He concentrated on looking forward to that; it would be exciting, and worth the long, nervous hours on the bus. Before long Pasang pointed through the window at a broad, brown river and the dingy buildings that surrounded it.

Tenzin stared, his face falling in disappointment. So this was the great city he had imagined? This ugly, smoky place? He said nothing as he stepped off the bus behind his brother. Pasang led him across the busy, noisy streets toward the biggest building Tenzin had ever seen: looming over them, a huge concrete-and-glass structure, its entrance flanked with Chinese statues.

"The train station," Pasang said.

Pasang bought two tickets, and they sat down together in the crowded waiting room. All around them jostled noisy families, business people and laborers, soldiers and severe-looking officials. Unsure how to act, Tenzin kept his eyes down.

"We'll have to wait here for a while. Are you hungry?"

Tenzin nodded.

Pasang bought two bottles with a fizzy, orange drink inside, and carefully divided up the biscuits they had packed. As Tenzin munched, Pasang discreetly pointed at someone waiting nearby.

"See that man there? And those two over there? They're all police."

Tenzin had already noticed a few uniformed police officers patrolling the station, but he'd had no idea that they could look just like regular travelers. And there were so many, all assigned to watch one station!

Pasang leaned closer. "You can always tell who the secret police are by their haircuts and neat clothes," he whispered. "Avoid catching their eye. Just look away. And never speak to them. If they find out we're trying to leave the country . . ." he paused slightly before adding, "they'll treat us badly. That's something I learned the hard way."

Tenzin looked up at his brother. He thought of the way Pasang had talked about his adventures, always seeming to hold something back. A shiver ran through him. As they finished their biscuits in silence, Tenzin made a decision. He would make a promise to himself, and keep it no matter what.

Pasang is brave, he thought, *and I must be, too.*

A loud hoot made him jump. "What was that?" he cried.

"*That's* a train," said Pasang.

There was a great clanking noise as the massive engine passed along behind the frosted windows of the waiting room. It was so loud Tenzin wanted to cover his ears—but he didn't dare; no one else was. An official held up a sign.

Pasang shook his head. "But it's not ours. We have to wait a bit longer."

Tenzin watched as people crowded through the narrow gate to the platform. The train left and the bustle quieted down, but Tenzin remained tense and still, afraid to relax. He noticed Pasang watching him.

"You know the time I ran away from the monastery?" his brother asked.

Tenzin nodded.

"I came here. I'd seen a train before, but I had no idea how to catch one, and I had no money. So I hung around for a couple of days, watching and listening, before I took a chance and jumped on one. I stayed on that train for three days and two nights." He shook his head and smirked at the memory. "Whenever the ticket officer came through the carriage, I hid in the toilets."

"What did you eat?"

"I was small like you, so people felt sorry for me, and gave me things to eat. Eggs, bread—food you can buy at the stations along the way."

"Where did you go?"

"I wanted to visit the Holy City of Lhasa. The monks had told me it was a place full of wonders—where pilgrims would give monks money. The train was traveling through hundreds of small villages, with lots of rice fields. But something didn't seem right: all the faces I saw were Chinese. When the train finally stopped, and everyone got off, I found I was in Beijing. I'd taken the wrong train. I'd gone the wrong way, all the way through China."

Tenzin was horrified. "What did you do?"

"You think Xining is big? Beijing is huge. I've never seen so many people in one place. Wide streets full of cars, bicycles, and people, people everywhere. Some buildings have many stories, with moving staircases inside them that can take you up and down. On the ground floor, there are doors that open by themselves. You don't have to push them."

Another loud hoot startled Tenzin. Someone was shouting. Pasang stood up.

"That's our train now. Let's go. And don't worry." He grinned and held out his hand. "This time I know where we're going."

Clutching their packs, they ran for the platform. Tenzin looked anxiously up and down the track. Only now did he realize how long and powerful the train was. Hundreds of people could travel on it!

"How fast will the train go?" Tenzin asked.

"Really fast. But, you know, even then you can put a drink on the table and it doesn't spill."

Tenzin shook his head. He didn't believe it. Pasang saw Tenzin's amazement and laughed.

They boarded the train, and after a few minutes it rattled and banged into motion, moving out of the station.

"Settle down," Pasang whispered. "We've got hours on the train. We're going to the last stop on the line, a place called Golmud. After that, Lhasa."

Tenzin nodded. He had so many more questions to ask, but he followed his brother's cue to stay quiet. He gazed out the window at the scenery rushing past, then looked at the other passengers. Most of them, he noted, were Chinese, and they ignored him.

The train went faster and farther than Tenzin had thought possible. He remembered that time, long ago, when he had left the village to visit Pasang in his monastery, before his brother had run away. This was totally different. Already he was farther from home than he had ever been, and the train kept hurtling forward, at a rate that made his head swim. The countryside flew past—hills, valleys, and villages became a blur.

Suddenly remembering Pasang's words, Tenzin put his orange drink gently on the table in front of him. He watched it, but it didn't fall off or spill, just as Pasang had said.

"See that!" Tenzin marveled.

The train screeched to a stop at a station. Outside, food sellers walked up and down the platform. Through the open window, Pasang bought some barley bread, bananas, and, to Tenzin's astonishment, some fish. It was deep-fried and served in paper. He handed the hot package to Tenzin. So Sangye was right!

"But we don't eat fish," Tenzin said, wrinkling his nose. "Mother said so."

"Ah," answered Pasang, "there's a special reason for that. Where we come from, when someone dies, they're buried in the cemetery, like father. But in some parts of Tibet, high up in the mountains, where the ground is rocky or frozen and there is no earth, people can't bury their dead. They have a 'sky burial.' That's when special monks cut up the bodies and put the pieces out for vultures."

Tenzin was quiet. He had never heard of such things. It seemed there was a lot that Pasang knew that he didn't, especially about Buddhism. At school, Tenzin had never been allowed to study it.

"After death," Pasang continued, "the soul has gone, so the body is an empty vessel that can be given to help other living creatures. In the mountains there's another custom when babies and small children die. The same monks cut up the bodies, and put the pieces in the rivers and lakes, so the fish can eat them. That's why mother says we don't eat fish. But none of that happens around here. I've eaten fish, and it tastes fine. Try it."

Tenzin looked down at the fish. He was very hungry. He hesitated.

"Just eat the white flesh," Pasang encouraged him, "and look out for the bones."

Tenzin tried to forget what he had just been told and tasted a small morsel. It was delicious. He pushed the rest into his mouth with his fingers.

Already the train had taken them far from familiar hills, and they were now crossing the high plain. For hours, they sped alongside a vast inland sea, where huge flocks of strange birds gathered. The landscape looked alien to Tenzin. Home was beginning to feel very far away.

"Pasang," he whispered as passengers dozed around them, "why do we have to go away?"

Pasang looked surprised, then thoughtful.

"If we leave, we can make something of our lives, do things we can't here. We can learn Tibetan, and even English if we want. Not just scrape by, and run scared from the Chinese police. At home there's no future for you. All the jobs go to the Chinese." Pasang's voice had grown heated, and louder. He seemed to catch himself.

"We want to make Mother proud of us, right?" he whispered. Tenzin nodded. Pasang patted his shoulder. "Now get some sleep."

➤

After two days, the train reached the end of the line at Golmud. As Tenzin stepped down onto the platform, a cold wind whipped against his cheeks and dust stung his eyes. It was a grim-looking town, and he hoped they wouldn't stay long. Most of the other travelers seemed to feel the same way; they were scuttling off as if in a hurry to get somewhere else quickly.

"This is a grubby place, isn't it?" said Pasang. "But we won't hang around. We've got at least another three days' travel before we reach Lhasa."

Pasang reached into his pocket, and started counting out his money. They had set off with 300 yuan, money their mother had made selling a sack of grain, but with the cost of the tickets and food, they now had very little left. Tenzin looked anxiously at the few coins left in Pasang's palm.

"Don't worry," Pasang said quickly. "We can hitch a ride to Lhasa. I know where we can get one."

He led Tenzin to a yard dotted with makeshift teahouses and lodgings for long-distance truck drivers. Tenzin trailed behind as Pasang spoke to one driver after another. At last his brother struck up a longer conversation with one of the men. Tenzin eyed him warily. The man stood listening to Pasang, hands tucked in his jean pockets, the collar of an old leather jacket turned up against the wind. After a while he nodded, and Pasang turned to Tenzin.

"We're in luck. He's delivering a load of onions and potatoes to Lhasa and he'll take us the whole way."

The driver signaled for them to jump into the cab, and Pasang threw their bags inside. Tenzin climbed in after his brother, still wary. At least it was a relief to get out of the cold wind.

The driver leaned forward, started up the engine, boosted the heater, and flicked on the radio. As he steered out of the depot, a song crackled over the speakers. Tenzin's face relaxed into a grin. He had heard it many times before on his mother's transistor radio, his family's prized possession. For the moment he forgot his fears, and started to sing along. The driver laughed. They listened to the radio for hours, bouncing on the seats as the driver swerved to avoid potholes and large stones on the road.

The route seemed endlessly empty as evening came and the truck climbed higher up the Tibetan plateau. Through the darkness, sudden flashes of light ahead startled Tenzin. But it wasn't lightning, as he'd feared, only the headlights of oncoming trucks. Lulled to sleep, he dozed in the cab as they drove through the night.

It was daylight when he rubbed his eyes and looked out again over the vast plains. He stared at the herds of yaks and the nomads riding on horseback. The great plateau seemed to go on forever. It was so different from his homeland of green fields and steep valleys, red earth and small villages. People back home lived in cozy houses; they didn't roam across a stark landscape, living in tents.

Here there were no trees, just grasslands and distant white-capped mountains. *Cold and empty,* thought Tenzin, and he felt a sharp pang for home. He gazed up at the huge skies. The great cloud formations looked to him like ghostly Mongol armies galloping on horseback across the plain, as they did in the stories his mother told him about their ancestors. A flash of color in the bleak landscape caught Tenzin's eye; they passed *chortens,* sacred Buddhist buildings with streams of prayer flags fluttering outward in the strong wind. The air grew colder, and Tenzin huddled closer to Pasang.

The truck crawled uphill through snowbanks and over high mountain passes. Pasang pointed out a sign that proclaimed they had reached Wenquan, "The Highest Town in the World." Tenzin was in no mood for celebration. His head ached, and he was gasping for breath.

"That's the altitude," said his brother. "The air is thin. You'll get used to it."

But it got worse. When they stopped to eat a bowl of noodles, Tenzin had to rush outside to be sick.

As he steadied himself against the wall, he felt a rising panic. *What if I can't go any farther?* he thought frantically. *Will Pasang send me back?*

He felt a hand rest lightly on his shoulder. "You're going to be fine." Pasang stood next to him, his voice reassuring. He held out a stick of sugar. "It's altitude sickness. Just suck on the sugar. If it doesn't work, I'll get you some garlic. It'll help."

Back in the cab, Tenzin fell fast asleep sitting up, his head lolling against his brother's shoulder, as the truck drove on through the night.

It was daylight once again when the truck driver pulled to the side of the road to let a long convoy of green military trucks pass. As they drew closer to the Tibetan capital of Lhasa, Tenzin spotted more and more Chinese soldiers. He noticed a buzz of activity up ahead. A unit of soldiers was marching by the roadside, their commander conducting some military exercise.

"Boys, keep your heads down," warned their driver, "and pray that the army doesn't stop us."

They ducked below the windshield, and the driver slowed down to pass between platoons of soldiers lining the road. Tenzin was too intrigued to stay down. Cautiously, he peeped through the side window. At once he froze in horror.

As the truck crawled past, Tenzin watched an officer kick a young soldier hard in the stomach. The man collapsed, howling. Tenzin wanted to look away, but found he couldn't. Soldiers on either side pulled the grimacing man to his feet. The officer kicked him again and again, shouting all the while. No one interfered; no one even reacted.

Tenzin's teachers had been harsh, even brutal at times, but he had never seen violence to a fellow human being like this in his life. He dropped back down below the window. When the truck had safely passed the area, he whispered to Pasang what he had seen. Pasang looked grim.

"Maybe it's best that you know," he said at last. "They're capable of all kinds of cruelty. When we get to Lhasa, there will be thousands of troops. I've heard that there are so many soldiers in Tibet, they could surround the whole country in a few days."

He put his finger to his lips.

"From now on, we must be extra careful."

CHAPTER 3

Beggars in the Holy City

Seven days and nights after they left home, Tenzin and Pasang reached the fabled city of Lhasa. Tenzin's excitement grew as the truck freewheeled down a valley toward the Tibetan capital. Pasang seemed to share his good mood.

"See the river here?" He pointed. "The driver says it's called Kyuchi, which means 'Water of Happiness,' and Lhasa is 'The Home of the Gods.'"

They passed a huge monastery, topped with white domes.

"That's the Drepung Monastery. When I first came here, I heard people call it 'rice piles.' The domes look just like piles of rice, don't they?"

But as they drove into the city, Tenzin grew nervous. He looked in dismay at the red Communist flags that flew above so many buildings. Even in this ancient and revered Tibetan city, the Chinese were clearly in charge. Everywhere he saw

38

Chinese troops—in trucks, patrolling the streets, or stationed in the city squares. His mind filled with the image of the young soldier beaten on the roadside, and he remembered his brother's words of warning. Instinctively, he reached under his shirt and touched the red cord of good luck that his mother had made for him.

The driver stopped the truck in a side street, and the two brothers thanked him and jumped down from the cab. Gathering up their bundles, they joined a group of travelers snaking in a line toward the city center. Tenzin felt a little safer and unnoticed among the crowds of people from all over Tibet who had come to pray at the holy temples. Shuffling forward among the pilgrims, monks, and nuns, he inhaled the sweet aroma of burning pine and juniper twigs, along with the earthy smell of travelers; a mixture of fire-smoke and human skin. He kept his head down until the column of pilgrims suddenly stopped. Looking up, Tenzin beheld a sight that left him breathless. He stared up in awe at the Potala Palace, a dazzling citadel built on a hill, towering over the city, gleaming in the sunshine.

"Tibetans built it over three hundred years ago," Pasang said, a note of pride in his voice. "Even today it's the largest wooden building in the whole world."

It seemed to float above the city, pointing up toward the bright blue sky. Tenzin craned his neck to glimpse its lofty rooftop, only to see the red flag of China fluttering over it. He had a sudden feeling that he had seen this place before. Then he remembered: at home they had used old newspapers to cover cracks in the inner walls. On one wall was a yellowing picture of the palace that was now soaring up before him.

Tenzin smiled; he had never imagined that he would see it in real life.

Around them, street photographers were taking pictures of visitors in front of the palace. Tenzin tugged at his brother's robe.

"Pasang, we *must* have our picture taken here. One day we'll be able to show it to Mother." He was afraid Pasang would refuse to spend the money, but, to his delight, Pasang nodded.

Side by side, they stood solemnly in front of the Potala Palace, Pasang in his red monk's robes, Tenzin still in his blue school jacket and trousers, while a photographer snapped their image. Tenzin turned back to the palace.

"Who lives inside?" he asked Pasang.

"It was built for our leaders, the Dalai Lamas. But our own Dalai Lama left after the Chinese invaded Tibet." Pasang lowered his voice. "We mustn't speak of him here. Someone may overhear you. Remember, there are spies everywhere."

The brothers walked up the two thousand steps leading to the main entrance of the Red Palace, the highest part of the Potala. Tenzin tried to count the steps at first; at last he gave up. They made their way through some of the hundreds of rooms, past relics, shrines, and images. Fascinated, Tenzin stared at it all, tugging Pasang's arm to show him each new thing that caught his eye.

"These are all holy objects," Pasang whispered, "so we'll get a blessing from them. It will help us."

Tenzin followed Pasang's example, reciting prayers and lying face down in devotion through the countless halls.

The hours passed quickly. By dusk, Pasang and Tenzin

found themselves in the central square of Lhasa, exhausted and hungry. Tenzin watched as Pasang counted the last of their coins; there wasn't enough left even to buy a meal. Tenzin's stomach growled. He looked fearfully around the square. It was getting dark; where would they sleep?

"Come on," said Pasang. He headed for one of the restaurants run by Tibetans, and in its back alley knocked at the kitchen entrance. A man in a dirty apron looked cautiously out, and Pasang asked meekly if he could spare any scraps or leftovers. The man stared at him and then down at Tenzin, and a look of pity passed over his face. He disappeared briefly, then returned and handed them two plastic bags. Tenzin peered inside as Pasang opened them; they were filled with cooked meat and vegetables. Crouching in a back street, they devoured their scrounged meal.

It was very dark now. Pasang found a quiet doorway. "We'll sleep here," he said. Seeing Tenzin's dismay, he added, "It'll be fine. We'll cover ourselves with our coats."

Tenzin settled in the doorway, huddling under his coat. The ground was hard beneath him. As he struggled to sleep, his mind filled with thoughts of home. He pictured longingly the room where his family slept together in winter, heated by a stove that stayed alight all night. He remembered the warm, comforting glow of the oil lamps, and his mother putting hot ash through a hole in an outside wall into the space beneath the raised brick floor to keep them cozy during the long, cold nights. The memories made Tenzin painfully homesick. More than anything, he yearned to see his mother.

Tenzin squeezed his eyes shut to hold back his tears, remembering his promise to himself. He didn't want Pasang to catch him crying. But he couldn't control the sobs that welled up inside him. He dozed fitfully through the night, and in the morning Pasang found him with a miserable, tear-stained face. But his brother said nothing as Tenzin wiped his eyes. Wearily, he roused himself and looked around at the filth revealed by the daylight.

"Hurry up," Pasang said curtly. "We've got to get moving." Tenzin thought he sounded annoyed. "The Chinese police round up homeless people. We can't be found here."

Pasang stood waiting, his eyes darting around, while Tenzin scrambled unsteadily to his feet. He was ashamed now of the tear stains on his cheeks. Maybe Pasang was angry at him.

Pasang took Tenzin gruffly by the hand and led him briskly toward the city center. After a while he slowed his pace, and his grip on Tenzin's hand grew less tense.

"Come on," Pasang said more gently, "I want to show you something." They were nearing the main Buddhist temple known as the Jokhang. Pasang stopped before a brick furnace, almost as tall as a man, with a large hole in the front and another on top, where pilgrims burned pine and juniper twigs to ward off evil spirits.

Pasang pointed to the hole. "When I first came to Lhasa, I slept in there," he said, sounding oddly proud. He looked at Tenzin's doubtful face. "I was small enough then to fit—I was just thirteen. I managed to sleep several nights inside. The police never thought to look in there. And it was warm."

Tenzin peered inside the dusty cavity; it reeked of soot. He realized that things could be worse. Tenzin pictured Pasang, younger and smaller, crouched in the hole. He had done all this before, Tenzin realized, but with a huge difference—he had been alone.

Tenzin took a deep breath. Pasang would never catch him sobbing again, he thought fiercely. He had made a deal with himself, and he would keep it. He wouldn't let his brother down.

"What are we going to do now?" he asked, trying hard to sound calm.

"Well, we can't go anywhere without money. So we're going to beg. You can see for yourself there are lots of pilgrims who'll give you money. That's why there are so many beggars here. I did it before. But we have to be very careful," he added sternly. "The Chinese throw beggars in jail, so you must stay with me always. Never wander off or the police will get you."

Tenzin's heart sank. He spoke almost no Tibetan or Chinese. Here, no one understood the dialect they spoke at home.

Pasang seemed to read his thoughts. "Don't worry, you won't have to talk much!" He crouched down, face to face with Tenzin. *"Moo zi jit de ro nang?"* he said slowly. "Now you try."

Tenzin repeated the sounds, but Pasang shook his head. He made Tenzin say it over and over until he was satisfied.

"Good, you're ready. Now you know all the Tibetan you need to survive."

"What does it mean?"

"It means, '*Can you spare me a few coins?*'"

Pasang led him to a spot in the central square, where pilgrims streamed by steadily. Tenzin felt a sense of panic as his brother walked away, but Pasang installed himself a little distance apart, still within his view. Tenzin watched him approach pilgrims with an outstretched hand. The first two brushed him aside; the third dropped something hastily into his palm before stalking off. Pasang turned to Tenzin and grinned.

Tenzin took a deep breath. It was his turn.

"*Moo zi jit de ro nang?*" he said timidly to a man in dusty clothes who'd clearly traveled far. The man ignored him and kept walking. Tenzin looked around. Maybe he should choose someone better dressed, with money to spare, he thought. More boldly this time, he blocked the path of a couple. The woman looked sympathetically down at Tenzin and tugged her husband's sleeve. With a reluctant expression, the man dropped some coins into Tenzin's cupped hands.

This is easy, thought Tenzin. As the day went on, he grew even bolder. He discovered that his small size and innocent-looking face made him more successful at begging than his older brother. When Pasang signaled for him to join him, Tenzin handed over his stash of coins and bills with a triumphant grin. Pasang carefully tucked their earnings away in his pockets.

Pasang used a few coins to buy tea, and they sat together, cradling the hot cups in their hands.

"Just be careful who you ask for change," he reminded Tenzin. "Watch for undercover police. They're here to find troublemakers in the crowds. You can spot them if you know how. They're always Chinese, and they wear dark glasses and new clothes."

Tenzin thought of his tactic of choosing well-dressed pilgrims and swallowed. He'd been lucky.

Pasang sipped his tea, but his eyes kept darting around

the square. Tenzin tried to follow his gaze, but he couldn't pick out anyone suspicious.

When evening came, Tenzin felt more hopeful this time. They must have earned enough to pay for a night's lodging! However, Pasang had other plans.

"We have to save as much as we can for our journey. We can't waste money on food or shelter."

Tenzin's face fell, but he bit his lip. This time he wouldn't grumble about the doorway. But Pasang pulled him in another direction. "We can't sleep in the same place two nights in a row," he explained. When the square began to clear, he chose a spot under the market stalls.

"Pasang," Tenzin whispered as they lay wrapped in their coats. "When you were in Lhasa before, did the police ever catch you?"

Pasang was silent for a moment. "Once, yes," he said. He turned over on his back and stared at the stall floor above them. "They rounded up a whole bunch of us in the square and took us away to a prison."

Tenzin shivered. He wanted to know more, but at the same time was afraid to hear it.

"All sorts of prisoners were there," Pasang said, "young, old, lots of monks. The guards showed no respect to the old men. They beat everyone, young and old, with sticks. Young ones, like me, had to work. They took us out in a truck to where they were building barracks for soldiers. We shoveled cement all day, then went back to our cells at night."

"How long were you there?"

"Weeks. One day I saw a few monks escape by climbing one of the walls. I tried to follow them, but I was unlucky. I got caught."

"Did they beat you?"

Pasang sighed heavily. "They tied me with my hands behind a pillar and kicked me," he said simply, then was quiet again. Tenzin waited.

"But you know, it just made me more determined to escape. A few days later I got another chance. It was in the evening, and we were sitting on the ground eating our watery soup when I heard two old monks whispering. Right away I wondered if they were planning something. Then I was sure I heard one of them say the word 'toilet.' I pretended not to notice, but later I went to the toilets and saw that some bricks in the wall had been dislodged. I pulled the bricks away, and it looked very possible to get through.

"My heart was pounding. I decided to go, right then and there. But when I pulled myself through I banged my head on a nail. Blood was all over my face, getting in my eyes. I kept going. As soon as I slipped outside and was on my feet again, I heard the barking of police dogs.

"There was no going back now! So I ran forward, wiping the blood out of my eyes as I went. I could still hear the dogs behind me, but their barking sounded farther away. I headed down a road that ran alongside the river. The next instant I spotted a man riding a bicycle toward me, heading for the prison. I was sure he was one of the guards who had tied me up and kicked me."

Tenzin's eyes grew wide in the darkness. "What did you do?"

"The only way to escape was into the water. But it was freezing, and the river was wide, and I can't swim. The bicycle was getting closer, and I had to make up my mind. The current looked strong, and I was sure I'd get swept away, so I just kept standing there.

"The rider was so close by then that I could see him clearly —and I realized he wasn't the guard at all. He just rode by me as if he didn't care who I was or what I was doing there. So I waited until it was dark and quiet, and then I started walking, all the way back to Lhasa, and found somewhere to sleep."

Pasang turned on his side to face Tenzin. "So that's why we have to be very careful who we talk to, and stay hidden at night. Okay?"

"Okay," Tenzin whispered. He felt a little awed by Pasang's story. And he suddenly felt a strong trust in Pasang that was comforting, even in this damp, awful place. What else had his brother survived that he'd never told him about? But Tenzin didn't ask any more. His eyelids were already heavy, and this time he slept deeply.

➤

"Wake up Tenzin. *Now!*"

Tenzin's eyes flew open. Pasang was shaking him. It was still dark, and Tenzin blinked, confused.

It took him a moment to remember where he was. They had been on the move for weeks now, begging and walking from one end of Lhasa to the other, hunting for new hiding places each night. Tenzin propped himself up and felt the damp stone wall in the dark. Then he remembered the dim back alley they had settled upon for the night.

"Listen!" Pasang commanded.

There were voices nearby, angry, and the sounds of a scuffle.

"It's the police," Pasang hissed in Tenzin's ear. "They're arresting beggars, and they're getting closer. Come on."

He hauled Tenzin to his feet and led him down the alley and around a corner. Pasang moved quickly and noiselessly, and Tenzin stuck close behind him, terrified of losing him in the dark. Coming out onto a broader street, Pasang broke into a run. Panting, Tenzin kept up, until at last his brother slowed his pace. It was quiet around them now; no voices at all. But Pasang kept moving, pulling Tenzin by the arm.

After an hour or more of wandering, Tenzin had no idea where they were. At last Pasang settled again in a back doorway. Tenzin collapsed next to him.

"We've been lucky so far, but I'm not waiting for our luck to run out," Pasang said, stroking his matted hair. It was nearly dawn; Tenzin could see his brother's face more clearly now. His eyes were wide and looked alarmed. "It's only a matter of time before the police catch us. I've been seeing more of them. Secret police in the squares, I'm sure of it. I thought I was imagining things, but now I don't think so. It's like we're surrounded. We can't wait any longer. We're leaving Lhasa."

"But you said yesterday we needed more money for our big journey," Tenzin said. He thought about the cloth shoes Pasang had just bought for him in the market to replace the ones that had worn out. He was sorry now to have spent the money.

"There's no time for that anymore," Pasang said impatiently. "What good will that do us if we get arrested and locked up? We're leaving."

"Over the Snow Mountains?"

"No. We'd need to pay a guide and buy supplies and warm

clothes. We don't have that kind of money. We'll go another way. A faster way."

At first Tenzin was relieved to hear there was a way to avoid the mountain journey. The prospect had always frightened him. But all the same, he felt a strange dread that he couldn't explain. *A faster way,* Pasang had said. That had to be better, right? *Trust Pasang,* he told himself, *he knows what he's doing.*

"Rest now," Pasang said, leaning back and closing his eyes. "We'll go as soon as it's daylight."

CHAPTER 4

In Enemy Hands

In the morning the brothers hitched a ride on a truck heading south to Shigatse, Tibet's second-largest city. From there, Pasang told Tenzin, they would walk south to the border with Nepal.

"But I thought we were going to India," Tenzin said, confused.

"We are—one step at a time," Pasang answered. "Crossing into Nepal is the first big step."

After brooding over their meager funds, Pasang was sure their best hope was a quicker, but riskier, dash across the border, rather than the daunting mountain trek he had made in his first escape. The main highway was the fastest place to cross the Tibet–Nepal border, but it was also the most heavily guarded by the Chinese, who kept a vigilant watch for Tibetans attempting to leave the country.

"I know of at least five army posts along the road," Pasang

explained, after the truck had dropped them and left them in its trail of dust. "Chinese soldiers check every vehicle and traveler. So once we get closer we'll have to walk away from the road, around the checkpoints."

They set off on foot. As they plodded, Tenzin gazed around him at the most barren terrain he had ever seen. There was little grass, no trees, and few people. Hours passed without him spotting a single human being. A lone truck roared past them, and Tenzin stared after it forlornly.

"Pasang, can we hitch another ride?"

"Every time we get a ride, there's a chance the driver might report us to the police. So we only do it when we have to. When we can walk, we walk."

Tenzin was downcast, but he didn't argue.

As the sun dipped in the sky, Tenzin staggered. Pasang paused to let him catch up, but Tenzin kept lagging behind. Finally his brother halted and let out an exasperated sigh. When a dusty truck rumbled behind them, he flagged it down. The driver pulled up and opened the back doors for them. Tenzin was nearly overpowered by the smell that emerged: the truck was carrying a cargo of garlic bulbs. But he was so relieved to rest his legs that he held his breath and climbed in with Pasang.

Now that he was off his feet, Tenzin realized how terribly hungry he was. Garlic bulbs seemed better than nothing. He stuffed a couple of them into his mouth. Soon the pain in his stomach was agonizing; he held his belly and groaned.

Barely an hour later, the truck reached its delivery point. *So soon,* Tenzin thought dejectedly. The brothers jumped down and continued their hike through the desolate landscape.

The sky began to darken, and Tenzin wondered where they would find shelter in this wasteland. Suddenly he heard far-off voices that startled him after hours of nothing more than the sound of the wind. Pasang pointed ahead. In the distance they could both see a glowing light. As they approached it, Pasang realized what it was.

"It's a tent, lit from the inside with oil lamps," he said.

"But who lives in a tent out here?" Tenzin asked.

"They must be nomads, *Drog-pa*. They roam the plateau looking for pastures for their yaks. Let's go and ask them if they'll give us some tea."

Tenzin's face brightened.

Ducking inside the yak-skin tent, Tenzin and Pasang were greeted with a warming sight. A nomad feast was under way. The revelers were not drinking tea; the smell of barley beer filled the air. The men beckoned to the boys to join them. Pasang quickly spotted the leader, a grizzled man with a worn face and long plaited hair, sitting close to the fire, making everyone laugh. Pasang shuffled forward, and asked if the two of them could have something to drink. The man eyed them warily, then turned to a young woman next to him and bellowed an order. Soon the boys were sitting next to the fire, drinking yak butter tea, eating mutton stew and bread. Tenzin was ravenous and devoured everything offered to him.

Pasang was eating too, but he sat upright and alert. Tenzin noticed that the grizzled man kept his eyes on his brother. He began to ask questions—about who they were, and where they were going.

Tenzin looked down, while Pasang invented vague answers. "We made a pilgrimage to Lhasa," he said. "Now we're going to visit family."

But the man wasn't satisfied. He persisted, and his friends chimed in. Tenzin glanced up at Pasang. He could see him reddening. He hoped he wouldn't lose his temper.

"Where did you say you're from?" someone else asked. In fact, Pasang hadn't told them at all.

Pasang leaned closer to Tenzin. "We need to leave," he hissed. "Now!"

The thought of abandoning the warmth of the fire brought Tenzin close to tears. "But it's dark," he protested weakly.

"Come on," Pasang barked, dragging Tenzin to his feet.

Outside, he gave way to his frustration. "Why can't people just leave us alone?" he stormed, pulling Tenzin forward as he went. "What do they care?"

The cool night air stung Tenzin's cheeks, flushed from the fire, but it seemed to calm Pasang down. He glanced down at his own hand clenching Tenzin's shoulder, and let go.

"Look, it's safer traveling by night," he said, his voice softer. "Those people were asking too many questions. I felt surrounded in there, and I had a bad feeling. We can't trust them."

Tenzin nodded. *Pasang must be right,* he thought. *He's survived danger before. He's more cunning than I am.*

They walked beneath the stars in silence. As they passed a mound of large rocks that blocked the wind, Pasang looked around.

"It's safe here. Let's get some sleep."

Tenzin crept behind the rocks and wrapped himself in his coat. He'd slept this way so often now that he was almost comfortable. His eyes grew heavy at once, and before closing them he gazed only briefly at Pasang, who was sitting up to keep watch, listening to the distant howling of a wolf.

➤

Fifteen days after leaving Lhasa, the brothers reached the border town the Chinese had renamed Zhangmu. Tibetan travelers still called it Dram; it was the last town on the road between Tibet and its southern neighbor, Nepal. The climate was a dramatic contrast to what they'd experienced on the high plateau. Here the air was dank and warm, the trees dense with foliage. Tenzin felt a mounting sense of excitement. *This is it*, he told himself. *If all goes well, this is where we'll escape.* Looking at Pasang's face, he could tell his brother felt it, too.

"When I decided to come home again, I came this way," Pasang explained. "A guide told me it was possible to sneak over the border back into Tibet. You dress like a Sherpa, one of the mountain people of Nepal. Then you cross in the middle of the day, when the border post is really busy. If they catch you, he told me, you claim to be Nepalese and say you work in one of the shops along the border. There were maybe fifteen of us, all trying to get back home.

"I thought my best chance was to cross at the front of the group and be one of the first ones to slip through. But I was the youngest, and the others pushed me to the back. The border guards started getting suspicious and called for reinforcements. The first ones made it, but I was caught."

"What did they do to you?"

"They threw a bunch of us in a cell. They beat us. Each day Chinese soldiers came and took a few more of the others away. I never knew what happened to them. After about two weeks, they came for me. They took me outside. I had no idea what they would do. They fingered their guns, but then I realized it was just to frighten me. They took me to the main road, pointed away from Dram toward Tibet, and told me never to come back. I walked to the next town.

"But ever since then I've realized the Snow Mountains aren't the only way out. If it's possible to sneak *in* to Tibet at Dram, then there's a good chance we can sneak *out*. When I was in that cell, some of the other prisoners told me it's possible to cross the bridge in the dead of night, because the guards often fall asleep."

Tenzin was quiet. It was rare for Pasang to tell him so much about his own escape, and he didn't want him to stop yet.

"I'm telling you this so you understand that I've learned a lot, things that can help us. Three important things, and they've saved us already. I know how to live without money, and I know to trust no one."

"What's the third thing?"

"When to run."

➤

As the brothers neared the border they passed a sign that proclaimed the road to Nepal the "Friendship Highway." But Tenzin could see there was little friendship on it for Tibetans. Up ahead the area was garrisoned by a large corps of Chinese troops, scrutinizing all travelers.

"Every choice we make now is critical," Pasang said. "We'll have one chance, so let's not rush it. Stick close to me."

Hanging back behind a car parked near the border crossing, the brothers waited and watched. Uniformed police were patrolling the streets, on the lookout for smugglers or illegal travelers.

"There are more soldiers here than when I came before, a lot more," Pasang said. He looked at the checkpoint on the bridge that spanned the river separating Tibet and Nepal. "And they have searchlights now," he added, as if to himself. Pasang glanced at the nearby Zhangmu Hotel. He nudged Tenzin and pointed out the men drinking tea at tables outside. "Plainclothes police," he whispered. Tenzin stared at them. They looked so relaxed and unconcerned. "I can see their guns," Pasang explained.

"What do we do?" whispered Tenzin, trying to control his alarm.

Pasang sat frowning for a moment. "Wait until it's dark. Then we'll try to cross."

When Pasang was satisfied they were unnoticed, he led Tenzin to a restaurant and ordered noodle soup. They slurped their food without talking. Outside, the patter of rain began. Their meal finished, they slipped back out and headed into the town.

"We'll wait for the streets to empty—and for the guards to fall asleep," Pasang said once they'd settled in a quiet doorway. Hours passed. Tenzin struggled to stay awake, staring through the rain, which was now pelting down. It was after midnight when Pasang finally nudged him.

"Come on," he whispered. "It's dark enough. Let's go."

Within minutes of stepping out of their shelter, Tenzin was soaked, his wet clothes sticking to his skin. Shivering, he crept behind Pasang, back through the now empty streets toward the bridge. There was no sound other than the steady, lashing rain. Noiselessly they made their way closer, moving stealthily along walls, pausing in doorways to listen for any movements in the town. Before them lay the river's fast-flowing black water, and across it the outline of the mountains in Nepal and the prospect of freedom.

Tenzin pulled at Pasang's shirt. "Look! There are guards there in the shelter," he whispered.

Pasang peered ahead through the rain. For an instant he hesitated. "Yes, but they'll be asleep by now."

Crouching, Pasang started to creep around the shelter. Tenzin followed close behind, his eyes wide in the darkness. The pounding of his heart seemed to fill his ears.

A shout suddenly pierced the drone of the rain. Tenzin didn't even look at Pasang; instinctively he threw himself to the ground, pushing his head into the dank soil, and lay still. His mouth filled with water from a puddle, but he didn't dare move.

Please let them not see us, he prayed silently. Next to him, Pasang lay motionless. The sound of footsteps drew closer. Another voice barked an order. A searchlight illuminated the sky, then swiveled in their direction.

Pasang sprang up, pulling Tenzin with him. But their eyes were blinded by the glare of flashlights. Tenzin could make out only the shapes of three guards rushing straight at them.

"Stop!" the men shouted.

Pasang put his hands in the air. The first guard to reach them delivered a sharp blow to Pasang's shoulder with his flashlight.

"Lie down!" he ordered. Tenzin dropped down on his back, next to Pasang. The guards circled them, shining the flashlights in their faces. One of them leaned over Tenzin. He was a swarthy man with protruding eyes.

"Where do you think you're going, little one?" he sneered. "So you think you are escaping, eh?"

Tenzin stared up in mute terror. Close to his head, the man's long black rifle pointed at him. Tenzin tensed his body, waiting for the shot.

"No," Pasang broke in, "we're looking for our friends."

Another guard crouched and slapped Pasang on the face. "Are you trying to be clever?"

He ordered them to empty their pockets and bags. Tenzin watched helplessly as the guards confiscated everything of value: Pasang's watch, their spare clothes—and all the money they had begged so slowly and painfully. One of the men caught Tenzin by the collar and dragged him to the outpost next to the checkpoint, where he threw him into a cell. Two other guards pushed Pasang in after him.

They could hear the guards talking outside, their words muffled. Tenzin looked beseechingly at Pasang. His brother's face was grim, and his eyes shone with alarm.

"What's going to happen to us?" Tenzin whispered, almost inaudibly.

"I don't know," Pasang said distractedly, glancing about him, as if an escape route might suddenly appear in the walls. "These people are very dangerous."

The door opened and the guards entered the cell. Tenzin stared at the object one of them held in his hand. He'd seen one before, in the hand of a Chinese guard in Lhasa. He remembered Pasang telling him what it was, and a chill seized his heart: it was an electric cattle prod.

The guard switched it on. The buzz of the baton was followed by a vicious stabbing pain as the instrument touched Tenzin's body. The torment was terrible. Briefly, the guard turned off the baton, only to force it into Tenzin's mouth. When he switched it on again, it burned, and then everything before Tenzin's eyes went dark. He saw and felt nothing more.

When Tenzin opened his eyes again, the guards were leaving, but he felt only dimly aware of them. He was overwhelmed at first by the pain in his mouth. Nearby, he heard Pasang speak. Tenzin turned toward him. His brother was battered, his clothing torn.

"I need my scriptures, and my flashlight," he pleaded weakly. "I have to pray tonight."

Tenzin cringed, waiting for the guards to strike his brother. To his surprise, they simply handed Pasang the books and photos they had confiscated. Then they left. Tenzin stared plaintively at Pasang, and whispered his name. But his brother remained slumped against the wall, too weak to move. Tenzin heard laughter in the guardhouse, and he could smell the guards' cigarette smoke.

Please, he thought, *please let Pasang be all right.*

Moments passed, agonizingly long, before Pasang roused and dragged himself closer to Tenzin.

"Are you okay?" he whispered.

Tenzin tried to move a little and winced. "I think so," he gasped. His mouth hurt, and he could taste blood. "I ache all over, but I don't think anything is broken."

They sat dazed for a moment longer. Then Pasang sat up with a jolt.

"Tenzin," he whispered, "they've left the door open."

"Have they?" Tenzin answered vaguely.

"Get up now. This is our only chance."

Together they scrambled unsteadily to their feet and slipped through the cell door. The guards remained in their room, with the door closed. No one emerged to challenge them. Outside, all was unlit and silent. Tenzin blinked in amazement. Was it possible no one was coming after them?

They were making good progress when the silence was broken by the barking of guard dogs.

"Run!" Pasang urged. "Run for your life!"

They hurtled down the road. Pasang veered off, and Tenzin shadowed him as he threw himself into a ditch. They lay still, and listened until the barking ceased. Pasang signaled to his brother to start moving again. Together they crawled into the rain-soaked forest by the edge of the bridge—still on the Tibetan side of the border.

"We can't do anything else tonight," Pasang whispered. "We'll stay here."

Tenzin nodded miserably.

"Pasang, what happened to you in there? After I fainted?"

Pasang looked away. "There's nothing you can do about it," he answered. "You just have to take the pain. But don't worry," he added. "I managed to roll away from the worst blows."

As the night deepened, they lay hidden in the thick foliage along the river. Tenzin examined the bruises and welts left by the cattle prod and recoiled in horror. Small, slimy creatures were sticking to his arms and legs. They seemed to swell in size as he watched. He had never seen anything like them before.

"Pasang, what are they?" he cried out in a panic. "There are . . . snakes everywhere! Let's get out of here."

Tenzin sprang to his feet, ready to run out of the forest, but Pasang grabbed his arm. From where they stood, they could see that the bridge floodlights had been switched on.

They were trapped between the creatures of the forest and the vicious border guards.

It was too much for Tenzin. "We'll never get across," he moaned.

"We'll have to stay here until it gets light, and then find a way over." Pasang's steady voice failed to calm Tenzin.

"I don't want to stay here with these snakes!" he wailed.

"They're not snakes, Tenzin. Look, they're leeches, and they suck your blood."

Tenzin gazed in disgust. On his bare leg was a fat, round leech swollen with feeding. He reached down to brush it off.

"Don't try to pull them off," Pasang said quickly. "They dig in under the skin. This is how you deal with leeches."

He pulled a small box out of his pack and struck a match. He singed the leech, and it dropped off. Carefully, he dealt with the rest one by one, while Tenzin continued to shake with fear. When it was over, Tenzin sat hugging his knees.

Pasang crouched down next to him. "Get some rest," he said.

The boys lay down in their wet clothes. After a few minutes, Tenzin broke the silence.

"Are there wolves or bears here?"

"No," Pasang muttered wearily. "Just snakes. Go to sleep."

➤

At dawn, the brothers carefully picked their way though dripping palm fronds and trailing vines down to the riverbank, where Pasang discovered a spot far enough from the border posts to avoid the attention of the guards. They stared at the river that flowed between Tibet and Nepal, thundering through sharp rocks. It presented a formidable obstacle. Tenzin watched a small black-and-white bird, hopping unconcerned from rock to rock; it seemed unaware of the torrent raging around it. Pasang dipped a cloth in the water and gently wiped away the dried blood from Tenzin's swollen mouth and face.

On the far Nepalese bank there were fishermen with rods and lines, and women washing clothes. Pasang waved at them. The Nepalis signaled back that they should not attempt to cross the river: it was too dangerous, and they would drown. The brothers looked at each other. Neither could swim.

There was no hope of escape this way. And the other, longer route—over the Snow Mountains—looked impossible now. They would need to hire a guide, and the guards had taken all their money. Pasang looked grimly across the churning water before turning his back on the border and walking away.

"Pasang, what do we do?" Tenzin pleaded, trotting to keep up.

Pasang stopped and stared ahead. Then he turned to Tenzin. "This is going to be difficult," he said slowly. "You won't like what I'm going to tell you."

Tenzin braced himself, but when the words came they still struck him like a hard blow.

"We have to go back to Lhasa and start over. We're going to have to beg for more money, buy more clothes, then try again. And we will have to climb over the Snow Mountains."

"Oh," Tenzin said softly. He found he couldn't say anything more. In his mind, the Snow Mountains loomed as high as the sky.

CHAPTER 5

To the Snow Mountains

If he didn't speak up soon, Tenzin felt as if he would burst. Sitting next to Pasang outside Lhasa's Jokhang Temple, he struggled to find the right words to convince his brother.

"Pasang," he blurted out at last, "can we just go home now? I mean, we've seen the Golden Buddha in the Drepung Monastery and been inside the Potala Palace, isn't that good enough? Can we go home and tell Mother about it?" He stopped as his voice caught, tears brimming in his eyes.

The brothers had been back in Lhasa begging on the streets for weeks now, scrounging money to replace what they had lost. But it was taking so long, and every day Tenzin lived in fear of the police, who seemed to be everywhere. He was sure he couldn't take any more.

Pasang's mouth pressed into a firm line as he listened. It was a moment before he spoke. "Look. I promised I would take you to India, so I will. I told Mother it was the only way that we'd be able to make something of ourselves. Don't you remember why we're leaving? Do you want to go back to being hungry and pushed around all the time?" Pasang paused, pushing at some pebbles with his foot. "And there's something else," he added.

"What's that?"

"In the end, I told her that if she didn't let me do it, I would give up being a monk." He looked at Tenzin. "Do you know why I became a monk in the first place?"

Tenzin shook his head.

"Before Father died, the last time I saw him he was sitting in our yard in the sunshine. They'd sent him home from the hospital because there was nothing they could do. His face that had been so ruddy was sallow and pale, and all his strength had faded. He called me over and said, 'When I'm gone, you'll be the man of the house. Promise me you'll look after the family.'

"I was terrified. How could I replace him? Father was so strong. I'd seen him plough and sow a whole field in one day! Mother had spent everything we had on his hospital treatment, and after he died, things got worse. She worked all the hours the light lasted in the fields. As soon as it was dark we went to bed because there was no oil to light the house. Even when we managed to get oil, we often had no matches, and I had to take a straw and go to a neighbor to beg for some fire.

"Then in the night I would see Father in dreams. I was scared I was going crazy, or that Father's spirit wanted to take me, too. One night I woke up and found myself in the wood on the hill, cold and barefoot. I'd been sleepwalking. Mother was so worried, she took me to see the diviner, a monk at the Kumbum Monastery. He listened to her and prayed to the deities. Then he said that I would die soon and rejoin Father, unless I became a monk."

Tenzin sat spellbound. His mother had never spoken of any of this to him.

"No one in our family had ever been a monk," Pasang explained, "but I knew that on holy days mother gave the monks money to say prayers for us. It looked to me like an easy life, taking money for praying. So Mother took me to the monastery and enrolled me as a novice. But it was not at all what I expected.

"I was apprenticed to an old monk, who treated me like an unpaid servant. He beat me when I didn't recite my prayers properly. Sometimes he punished me for no reason at all. I ran home more than once, but Mother always took me back. In the end I decided that I would have to run far, far away. That's when I left Tibet the first time."

Pasang stopped suddenly. "That's more than I meant to tell you."

They sat in silence, basking in the last rays of the sun that lit the square. It would be dark soon. Instinctively now, Tenzin stirred; it was almost time to search for shelter.

But Pasang did not move yet. "So," he concluded, "that's why Mother let me take you with me. I told her it was the only way I would stay a monk. And that I promised Father to take care of you. And this is the best way I know how. That's why we're not turning back."

Tenzin fell still and stared forlornly down at his worn shoes, the ones Pasang had bought him at the market the first time they were in Lhasa. They were as tattered as his old ones now. He could see by his brother's stubborn expression that his mind was set. How could he possibly tell Pasang that he'd lost hope? He didn't want to go to India anymore; he didn't want adventures—he just wanted to go home. But if what Pasang said was true, he couldn't do that either. He squeezed his eyes shut to keep the tears from escaping. Pasang mustn't see.

A voice behind Tenzin made him jump.

"Hey, is that you, Pasang?" It was a friendly voice—something Tenzin hadn't heard for a long time.

Pasang swung round. He smiled with recognition.

"Ngawang! What are you doing here?"

A young man, a little older than Pasang, stood grinning at them. Tenzin stared at him. He was smaller than his brother, wiry, with a face that creased in folds when he smiled.

"Tenzin, this is my friend Ngawang. He was a monk in my monastery in India." Pasang's face beamed with happy surprise.

They bowed toward each other, touching foreheads, a mark of mutual respect.

"How about a cup of tea?" Ngawang suggested.

Together they visited a nearby tea stall, and soon they were settled together, cupping hot drinks in their hands. Tenzin winced as he sipped; hot tea still hurt his mouth, scorched by the electric baton. He eyed Pasang's old friend nervously. It had been so long since they'd sat like this with anyone.

Ngawang leaned in closer. "I've just come over the Snow Mountains," he confided, lowering his voice, "back to Tibet to see my family."

Tenzin watched Pasang hesitate. Then he appeared to make a decision.

"We're trying to make the same journey," he whispered, "in the other direction."

Ngawang sat back and nodded. "Ah."

Tenzin relaxed; Pasang must trust him.

"You'll need a guide." Ngawang added thoughtfully, "I know someone who can help you." He looked sympathetically at Pasang's and Tenzin's tattered clothing. "I can lend you some money, if you need it."

Pasang looked gratefully at his old friend; he seemed to be at a loss for words.

"Don't think anything of it." Ngawang waved his hand, trying to make light of it. "I've had some rich sponsors pay me for prayers lately!"

Things began to happen quickly. The next morning Ngawang introduced them to the guide. He was a stocky man, not tall, but strongly built, with a weathered face. And he wasted no time.

"Six hundred yuan—each," he said curtly, after looking the brothers up and down.

"We have no money, only what we can beg!" Pasang protested. "You must be able to make it cheaper for us."

This time Tenzin was glad of his brother's stubborn streak. At last the guide agreed on a sum of three hundred yuan for both of them. He told them that the next few weeks would be the best time of year to climb over the Snow Mountains. The monsoon season had ended, and winter's harsh weather and freezing temperatures were not yet making the journey too hazardous. They arranged to meet again in a hostel in Shigatse in a few days.

"Just think," Pasang encouraged Tenzin, "last time we walked on our own most of the way from Shigatse to the border, but this time we'll have a guide to help us."

Tenzin caught some of his brother's enthusiasm. Soon they would be leaving Lhasa and its police for good—that was something, at least. It was better not to think too much about the mountain journey for now, Tenzin decided, or too much about the future at all.

In Shigatse, they found the hostel in one of the city's back streets. It was a shabby place. Tenzin looked around apprehensively as they opened its crooked door; everything about it looked neglected, as if people came and went in a hurry, not bothering to look back. Several other people were already waiting inside the entrance hall. Some were wearing monks' robes; others were already bundled up in warm clothing. But they all had the same expression, solemn and determined. Beyond them, Tenzin spotted their guide, who waved them over.

"What you must do now is gather the supplies you need— especially extra clothing and food. But make sure to avoid the police. It's going to be a tough journey, so get as much rest as you can. Now wait over there with the others. I'll have more to tell you."

"Which route are we going to take?" asked Pasang.

"There's no need for you to know yet. You'll find out soon enough."

Tenzin noticed a girl sitting nearby, smiling shyly at Pasang. She looked about the same age as his brother. Pasang and Tenzin took the empty chairs next to her, and they started talking. Her name was Pema, and she looked relieved to confide in someone.

"I'm so nervous—about the mountains, the border guards," she said, talking quickly, "but if you get to see the Dalai Lama, it's worth all the suffering, isn't it?"

Tenzin concentrated hard to follow her rapid words. Pasang had taught him more Tibetan since their journey had begun, but it was still a struggle for him.

Pema looked at Tenzin and smiled again. "If I return home and can tell people that I have seen His Holiness, I'll have no regrets."

The guide was hovering nearby. "No talking more than necessary!" he barked. "Don't tell one another about yourselves. If anyone is caught by the Chinese border guards and interrogated, no one must be able to give away information about the others. Understood?"

Pema flushed and lowered her eyes.

Tenzin looked around and counted the refugees: twenty-four in all. He was by far the youngest. A wave of anxiety swept through him. *What if I can't keep up?* He said nothing to Pasang. He'd promised himself that he would be brave. But inside, his terrible doubt kept growing.

➤

The truck bounced along the rough road, pitching its human cargo from side to side. Enclosed in darkness, Tenzin could see nothing, but he felt overwhelmed by the crush of people. He panted for air in the hot, stifling atmosphere. Around him, most of the refugees were standing, while Tenzin crouched down on his haunches, listening to the low whispers over his head. He caught little of what people were saying, but they sounded both anxious and exhilarated.

Suddenly their driver shouted, "Everyone, silence!"

Moments later the truck slowed to a halt. Tenzin strained his ears in the dark. He could hear a commotion outside the truck. Next to him, Pasang whispered, "We're at a police checkpoint. Those are soldiers shouting!"

The driver hollered back at the guards. Tenzin froze. He pictured the back door of the truck being thrown open, and everyone discovered and arrested. It could happen at any moment. Around him the other fugitives held their breath. He closed his eyes tightly. Water fell on his head, trickling down his face, but he didn't dare move. The moisture stung his eyes; he realized it was cold, salty sweat dripping off the man directly above him. Eyes still shut, Tenzin prayed to the deity of his village, and then to the Buddha.

Please, let us be safe. And let me go home and see Mother again.

He felt a jolt. The truck slowly moved forward. Everyone around him began to breathe in relief again. So far, the guide was fulfilling his promises.

A few hours later, the truck halted once more. The back door swung open to reveal the guide's face.

"You've got ten minutes. Then it's back in the truck."

Tenzin and Pasang jumped down with the others, some immediately disappearing behind trees. Tenzin covered his eyes at first, unused to the bright sunlight. Then, squinting, he saw that they were on a remote stretch of road. When he looked up he gasped. Soaring above them was the Himalayan mountain range—the greatest peaks in the world, he'd heard the others say. So here at last before him were the Snow Mountains.

He had glimpsed them from a distance on their way to Dram. But back then he and Pasang had expected to cross the border at the river, and Tenzin had given the mountains little thought. Now that he faced the prospect of crossing them, they looked impossibly high. How could he ever climb this massive barrier? And it seemed he wasn't the only one who felt that way.

"You never told us!" someone exclaimed in horror.

Another man grabbed the guide's arm. "How are you going to get us over?"

More alarmed voices chimed in.

"Oh, it will only take a few days to climb over," the guide reassured them. He spoke confidently, almost casually. "Don't worry. Hundreds do it every year."

Tenzin saw Pema and another girl exchange doubtful looks. He could tell that no one believed it would be that easy.

➤

After several more hours on the road, the truck stopped again. The driver called back to his passengers.

"This is where the road ends. Everyone out!"

The back door opened. It was night now, but Tenzin could still make out the peaks overhead, and even a village in the middle distance.

"Be as quiet as you can," the guide whispered as he helped the refugees off the truck. "Go hide down there behind the rocks. I'll check that it's safe."

Tenzin crouched next to Pasang and waited for the guide's signal. The burly man waved the group over and, one by one, they followed behind him in a line, stumbling along in the dark. From his first steps, Tenzin felt almost sick with fear. Even Lhasa was better than this—walking blindly into the unknown. He had to hurry just to keep pace with Pasang.

After a few hours they reached the snow line. Tenzin looked down at the outline of the village, already far below them. And they would have to climb much higher.

Tenzin's throat was parched with thirst. He bent down and scooped snow into his mouth. Looking up at the mountains, a panorama of shadowy, awesome presences, he felt a flood of panic. It was simply impossible that they were going to climb over them. Just keeping up was already exhausting him. Once again, he felt overwhelmed with homesickness. *I want to see Mother again,* he thought. *Nothing else matters.*

Tenzin pulled Pasang's arm. "Can we go home?"

"Of course not," Pasang snapped. The rebuke was like a slap. "Remember," he added, more patiently this time, "I've climbed over the Snow Mountains before. It wasn't here, but farther west, near the Sacred Mountain. I know you can do it."

Pasang shouldered Tenzin's bundle.

"Let's go."

Tenzin followed; he had no choice. All he could do was move forward, and try not to think about what might happen. He trailed behind Pasang, steadily putting one foot in front of the other.

CHAPTER 6

Toward the Death Pass

Tenzin clung tightly as the guide carried him on his back, wading across the icy river. He glanced down at the churning water and prayed the guide wouldn't lose his footing. Looking up, Tenzin focused next on Pasang's back, moving ahead of him. His brother's legs were almost entirely underwater. When at last Tenzin clambered down safely on the far bank, their guide allowed the group only the briefest of rests. They risked freezing to death whenever they stopped moving.

"Check your hands and feet for frostbite," he reminded them before they set off again. "Rub your fingers and toes hard. You might lose them if you don't."

Tenzin opened and closed his fingers, staring at them worriedly. He shivered in his thin canvas shoes, jeans, and jacket. The clothes he and Pasang had bought in Shigatse were wretchedly inadequate for this cold. Pasang had given him their quilted blanket to wrap around his shoulders as he walked, but the wind still cut through. Tenzin inspected his feet: his sneakers from the Lhasa market were ripped now. His feet looked swollen, and he had cuts. He rubbed them, and then, pulling his blanket around him, jumped up to follow the others, who had started to walk again.

Tenzin was grateful that at least his wool hat protected his head and ears. Pasang had exchanged his monk's robes for heavier clothing, but his baseball hat did little to warm his head. Ahead of them, Pema and her friend Dawa walked together, gloveless hands shoved in their pockets. All trudged in silence, concentrating on the effort needed to steady themselves on the steep slopes, where loose stones tumbled downward with each step.

Pasang walked close alongside Tenzin, clutching his arm whenever he was in danger of slipping on the icy terrain. Tenzin shuddered to think what would happen if he fell and was injured up here and couldn't go on.

"Pasang, isn't this the way you went before?" he asked.

Pasang shook his head. "I told you, that was farther west. This is higher and . . . colder." He broke off.

Ahead, a young man bundled in heavy clothes looked back at them.

"Have you guessed yet which way our intrepid guide is taking us? We're going to cross the Nangpa-la—the high pass near Mount Everest. Have you heard of it?"

Pasang frowned and glanced at Tenzin. "Let's save our breath," he answered.

But the man ignored the hint. "They call it 'the Death Pass.' No one knows how many people have died up there. If we don't freeze to death, the Chinese border guards will use us for

Brothers Tenzin (11) and Pasang (19) were raised in northeastern Tibet.

© *Mike Shrimpton*

Tenzin worked in the fields, often as a shepherd.

© *Mike Shrimpton*

The family home lacked electricity and running water.

© *Nick Gray*

The boys' mother worked long hours to support her family.

© Pasang/Tenzin

Pasang, in novice monk's robes, and Tenzin, in school uniform, pose in front of the Potala Palace in Lhasa, the Tibetan capital.

© Pasang/Tenzin

Pema and Dawa, two of the refugees who befriended Tenzin.

© Mike Shrimpton

Tenzin (center) wrapped himself in a quilt on the ascent to the Death Pass over the Himalayas.

The escapers rested on the glacier at the Tibet–Nepal border, where the temperature averages −20°C (−4°F).

By the time they arrived in Dharamsala, India, Tenzin and Pasang were exhausted.

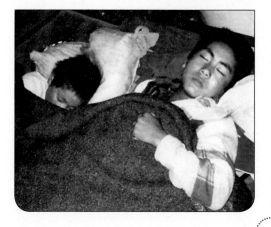

His Holiness the Dalai Lama welcomed everybody including (front row, left to right) Dawa, Pema, Pasang, and the 'old man' Tsering.

© ITV-Yorkshire

Tenzin, his head shaved, on his first day in the Buddhist monastery in southern India.

© Pasang/Tenzin

At the British High Commission in Delhi, the brothers display visas that will allow them to start new lives in England.

© Nick Gray

target practice with their long-range rifles." He let out a mirthless laugh like a bark before turning to face ahead once more.

Tenzin looked anxiously at Pasang, who was glaring at the man's back.

"If you hear shots," Pasang said quietly, "throw yourself on the ground and crawl behind the rocks. Hide there and don't move."

They had been walking for three days. Now the path rose steeply before them; the snow underfoot was frozen solid. Tenzin wondered why, when the sun was so bright, it never warmed them and the snow never melted. Sparkling in the dazzling light, the white crust lay hard under his feet.

"The border with Nepal is at the top of the pass," the guide announced. When he told them it was almost 19,000 feet, everyone looked up, as if trying to calculate how long it would take to reach it.

"Just keep walking," their leader urged. "You can't see the pass. We will reach it tomorrow, maybe."

Tenzin was relieved when at last they stopped for another rest. But Pasang sent him to gather twigs or yak dung, if he could find any, to start a fire. He had started the journey carrying forty pounds of *tsampa*, toasted barley, in his backpack. The brothers had begged for it in Shigatse, going door to door in the Tibetan community. Ground into meal, it was now their survival food. If they could heat some water, Pasang could mix it with tea and yak butter and make a kind of porridge.

But the guide overheard their plans. "What are you doing?" He blocked Tenzin's way. "There are border guards around here. They'll spot the smoke!"

Tenzin squatted next to Pasang, who wet the barley with snow, squeezing it into balls in his hands for them to eat. Pasang pulled a little rock sugar and garlic out of his backpack and gave Tenzin some.

"To ward off altitude sickness," he said.

As he chewed, Tenzin watched his brother dig through his pack. Along with the *tsampa*, it was stuffed with a second blanket, their spare clothes, as well as Pasang's Buddhist scriptures and family photos. Buddhism and family were both very important to Pasang. It was a heavy load, Tenzin realized.

I have enough trouble keeping up, and all I'm carrying is my blanket, Tenzin thought. He'd kept quiet, but a grim certainty had been growing inside him. He wasn't going to make it over the mountains. He looked at Pasang, who sat resting, his shoulders heaving wearily.

"Pasang," Tenzin said in a small voice, "am I going to die on the mountain?"

Pasang glanced sharply at him. "No, no," he said quickly. "Hundreds cross the Snow Mountains every year. Lots are children."

Tenzin couldn't believe it. "Someone my age has made it before?"

"Sure," replied his brother. "I met lots of them in India. Even babies are carried over the mountains in their parents' arms. That's why I know that you can do it."

Tenzin was about to answer when he noticed the shadow of someone standing over them. It was the young man who had told them about the Death Pass. He crouched down next to Pasang and nodded. He glanced at Tenzin, and his long, serious face almost moved into a smile. Maybe he was sorry to have frightened him.

Their guide had often repeated his order to keep talking to a minimum. But Tenzin noticed that the farther they trekked up the mountains, the more relaxed everyone became about this rule. Pasang and the stranger fell into conversation.

The young man's name was Sonam. He was dressed warmly, like a Sherpa, but he showed Pasang what he was carrying in his pack—the red robes of a Buddhist monk. He was going to India so he could practice his religion, but there was another more pressing reason.

"I had to leave in a hurry," he told Pasang, "because the police are after me."

Sonam had encouraged his fellow monks to resist the Chinese, stirring up rebellion in his monastery. Now the troublemaker was a fugitive. In Pasang, he seemed glad to have found a new audience to recruit to his cause.

"You know, since they invaded, the Chinese have destroyed more than two thousand monasteries." Sonam's lean face grew animated as he talked. "There are now only eighty thousand monks in Tibet. Before the Chinese came, there were more than half a million! I complained about what was happening in the monasteries, and spies reported me to the police."

Undeterred by warnings, Sonam and a few like-minded monks had waited until nightfall, then crept out of the monastery. In the center of the town, they put up posters that read "FREE TIBET." Sonam grinned with pride at the memory.

Pasang said nothing, but Tenzin could tell he didn't approve.

Sonam didn't seem to notice. "The next day," he continued excitedly, "three or four jeeps drove up to the monastery.

Soldiers got out, with guns at the ready, and their commander called an immediate meeting with all the monks. 'I want to know who put up the posters,' he shouted. 'We know that monks from this monastery did it. We will find out who they are, and they will be executed.' They picked out several of us for interrogation, and of course I was one of them. They threw me against the wall, demanding to know if I had anything to do with the posters. I denied it. They put me in prison, and said that I would be executed. But with no evidence and no confession, they had to release me. From that moment I knew they were watching me all the time.

"I decided it was too dangerous for me to stay. So I put on peasant's clothes and joined this lot," he said, waving his hand at the refugees huddled around them. He pointed to a tall man nearby. "My cousin Rinchen is with me. He has nothing to keep him in Tibet. The Chinese confiscated his farm."

"What will you do when you get across?" Pasang asked.

"We want to meet the Dalai Lama, and maybe settle in one of the Tibetan communities in India, if we can. Rinchen can farm, and I'll find a monastery."

Pasang shared a little of his own story, and of his plans for himself and Tenzin, without revealing too much. Sonam took out his holy books and, a little way off, started praying on the mountainside.

Pasang nudged Tenzin. "Look." He pointed out Sonam's quilt jacket. It had some new stitching at the edge. "I'll bet he's sewn money into the lining to hide it from robbers and border guards . . . and from any other prying fingers," Pasang added, looking around at their group.

"Sonam must be very brave," Tenzin said.

"Hotheaded is more like it," Pasang answered. "He's been reckless. I'd never put us in that much danger."

The guide waved them forward; it was time to move on. This time Pema fell into step alongside Tenzin and offered him some of her food. Tenzin quickly felt at ease with Pema, with her open, sympathetic manner. *This must be what an older sister is like,* he thought. He noticed Pasang watching them, smiling.

Tenzin looked up at Pema's delicate face, shaded by the baseball cap she always wore. She had seemed so frail in the hostel, but she was proving to be tough and determined on the mountain. She had been a waitress in Lhasa, she told Pasang and Tenzin.

"I mostly washed dishes," she admitted. "Before that I worked as a hairdresser."

"Why did you decide to escape?" Pasang asked her.

"I'm not at all political," Pema said, shaking her head. "It really all happened by accident.

"Four of us had an evening off, so we decided to go to the movies. On the way there we saw men in the street shouting slogans—'Free Tibet' and things like that. They were holding placards, demanding independence from China. We didn't want to get involved, so we just ignored them, and hurried into the movie theater. When we came out, there was a full-scale riot going on. Chinese police were chasing people down the streets with electric batons.

"There was a policeman just near us, and in the heat of the moment one of my friends picked up a stone and threw it at him. The police started chasing us. We ran, but I tripped and fell. The police caught up and arrested me."

At gunpoint, Pema was herded along with the protestors into a truck and driven to the main police station in Lhasa's Barkhor Square. They were thrown into a crowded cell and held overnight. The next day Pema's family learned of her arrest. Her uncle, a civil servant working for the Chinese government, rushed to the police station and used his influence to get her released. When he took her home to her parents, he denounced her as foolish and ignorant.

"He was yelling and waving his arms about," she continued. "He shouted at me: 'Why did you get involved? Don't you understand? I'm a government official. I could get fired because of you!' He told me he could even be sent to prison because of what I'd done. He really humiliated me. My mother joined in, scolding me. She told me that as I had no idea what Tibetan independence meant, I should have nothing to do with it."

In the end her uncle had kept his job, but to save her family from any danger, Pema had planned her escape from Tibet. She'd told no one, not even her parents. But she had wanted them to know why she was leaving, so she wrote a letter to her mother.

"I told her that in India I would learn so much more. I didn't want to stay in Lhasa, and be treated as a second-class citizen. It's hard to get any kind of job, and even harder to keep it. The Chinese get all the best jobs. I wrote that if I went to India, I'd get some education. When I return home, I can do something more useful, maybe get a better job. I don't want to be a waitress all my life."

"That's not so different from us," Pasang agreed. "A chance for something better—that's why we're going, too. I'll go back to my monastery in the south of India, in Karnataka. Tenzin will go there too, to learn Tibetan and English—he's very clever."

Clever, Tenzin thought with wonder. *I didn't know Pasang thought I was clever.*

"At home I felt like I was walking a tightrope," Pasang went on. "The Chinese control everything, and they have spies in the village. If I make the slightest mistake I know that they'll confiscate everything our family has and send me to prison. Where we live, the local police treat us like animals." His voice had grown angry; up ahead, a few heads turned to glance at him. Pasang fell silent.

"Is this hard for you?" Pema asked tentatively after a moment. "I mean, this journey, the walking, the cold, everything?"

Pasang shrugged.

"It's very hard going for me," she confided. "At the start, I got scared by stories of refugees who fell down ravines because they lost their balance under heavy loads. So I just abandoned most of what I was carrying."

"That was probably smart," Pasang said, encouragingly.

"You and Tenzin are lucky to have each other. To watch out for each other, I mean. Dawa and I have promised to look out for each other. It makes you feel a little braver, safer, you know?"

Pasang paused a moment. "We'll watch out for you too," he said after a while.

Tenzin began to fall behind as Pasang and Pema talked. He looked backward and was surprised to see he wasn't the last one.

He tapped his brother's back. "Pasang," he whispered loudly, "I think there's someone who's even slower than me."

Pasang turned to look at the haggard fellow who lagged a little distance behind them. "Oh, the old man?" he said.

The man raised his eyes and glared at Pasang. His wrinkled, sunburned face scowled. "My name is Tsering and I'm not that old, maybe forty-something," he protested loudly.

The way forward grew more treacherous. Worst of all were the steep scree slopes. Pasang and Tenzin slid dangerously, their thin-soled shoes giving them no grip on the loose stones. They crossed a glacier that extended like a flat ocean, and made their way over rivers of ice, their guide checking for hidden crevasses with a stick. Tenzin struggled to keep up, all the time thinking that at any moment the ice could give way, and any one of them could fall through. As they climbed higher, the bone-chilling wind seemed to increase, biting through his flimsy clothing, blasting him at every step. And the guide moved relentlessly forward, constantly urging them on.

Tenzin kept staring at Pasang's back, moving steadily ahead of him, and thought of home, of his mother. He remembered the red blessing string he still wore under his shirt—was it strong enough to protect him now?

If only I was sure I would see her again, he thought, *I could keep going.*

At this time of year his mother would be leading the family out to harvest the crops. Tenzin imagined the scene: the grown-ups cutting the wheat and barley, the mounting piles of potatoes and broad beans. Most of what they grew had to be sold, and soon the truck would arrive for the men to load with the harvest. They would all be carrying flasks of the black, salty tea that kept hot all day. Tenzin would have given anything to taste that tea just then. He could picture, so clearly, his mother carrying a bundle of wheat, smiling at him. He held the image of her face in his mind.

A large black bird soared overhead. Was it an eagle, or a vulture? *That lucky bird can fly over the mountains in a few minutes,* Tenzin thought, *but for me it's taking forever.*

➤

Tenzin glanced down as he passed a dead yak, perfectly preserved, frozen in ice and snow.

How many other bodies are buried in the snow and ice here? he wondered. *How many people have died on this journey?*

They had been walking for five days now, seldom stopping, sleeping for only snatched half-hours, the brothers huddling together for warmth. As they halted for another brief rest, this time their guide hacked a pile of frozen yak dung out of the snow and made a fire with it. He filled a pot with snow, and soon there was hot tea for all.

Pasang looked at the smoke from the fire and told Tenzin to keep his eyes open. "I've heard of Chinese army units operating even at these high altitudes," he said quietly.

Pasang reached into his pack for their dwindling supply of *tsampa* and noticed Tsering hovering nearby.

"It's very hard on me," Tsering was complaining to anyone who would listen. "I am stiff, and get tired easily."

He seemed eager to share his story, and he told Pasang that he was leaving Tibet because he and his parents had lost everything. They had fallen behind in paying their taxes, and the Chinese authorities had claimed their property and livestock, and driven the family from their home. His parents had died, Tsering said, of broken hearts. Tsering himself had taken to the road, and learned how to survive there. He boasted about how successful he was at begging for money and food.

"He's certainly always around when any food gets unpacked," Pasang muttered to Tenzin.

Tsering showed them a treasure he carried with him. Carefully, he unwrapped a carved bone, a memento of his mother.

"When I meet the Dalai Lama, I will ask him to bless this bone," he said. "Then I will know my mother's spirit is at peace."

Once Tsering had ambled away, Pasang whispered to Tenzin, "Keep an eye on him."

"What do you mean?"

"Just that if any money or food goes missing," Pasang answered, "we'll know where to look."

Tenzin nodded. As he sipped his tea, he watched the guide turn to the mountain and kneel.

"He's praying to the god who is the keeper of the pass," Pasang said. "The god will decide if we cross or not. See over there? That's the highest mountain in the world, so he may be praying to her, too."

Towering above them was the summit of Mount Everest, straddling the border between Tibet and Nepal. Tenzin gazed up at the peak Tibetans revered so much they called it Chomalongma, "Mother Goddess of the World." The cold was so intense that Tenzin felt numb as he stared. He knew they would be on their way soon, blundering upward. His eyelids felt heavy, and he let his head fall forward as he slumped next to Pasang.

He felt Pasang shaking him hard.

"You're falling asleep! Get up! If you get left behind you'll freeze to death."

Tenzin rose and stumbled onward. The guide was already far ahead, the others staggering behind him in a line, toward the highest mountain pass in the world.

They now faced the toughest challenge of the trek. As they climbed ever higher, the temperature fell so far below freezing that Tenzin's throat and lungs hurt from the biting air. And he felt breathless, always panting to draw enough air in. Every few minutes, he stopped to catch his breath, while Pasang halted to let him catch up.

"At this altitude, there's less oxygen," Pasang explained as he waited, his words emerging in gasps. "That's why you're panting."

Tenzin remained bent over, unable to answer.

"You know, in the monastery," Pasang added, "our teachers say a true Buddhist needs to experience this kind of suffering to increase his wisdom and compassion."

Tenzin raised his head. "All I can think about is staying alive."

"You're right." Pasang nodded as they moved forward together. "You don't contemplate wisdom when you're struggling to survive."

Suddenly a shout up ahead made them stop in their tracks. The guide was waving, then pointing to something ahead of them. Pasang looked alarmed. He motioned to Tenzin to stay put while he moved forward to see better. Tenzin waited, wondering what new danger they had walked into. He thought about the army units. They were on an exposed snowfield with no cover. Then Pasang turned to him with a shout.

"I think it's the border!"

CHAPTER 7

The Fateful Step

Tenzin caught his brother's excitement, and felt a surge of energy. They set off again, a new vigor in their stride.

Ahead, Tenzin could make out a cairn of piled-up *Mani* stones, special slates carved with Buddhist prayers. Leading out from the stones were strings connecting hundreds of fluttering, colored flags with Tibetan prayers printed on them, the wind carrying the prayers to all parts of the world. They had reached the highest point of their journey: 19,000 feet. Word passed quickly through the group: the cairn marked the border with Nepal. The news raised the spirits of the refugees. They were about to leave Tibet! As they neared the border cairn, Pasang and Sonam both raised their arms and cheered.

"*Lha Gyalo!*" they shouted.

"What are you saying?" Tenzin called. "What does it mean?"

"It's a prayer: 'May the gods be victorious!'"

Tenzin looked back. He could see little sign of what he was leaving behind, his country, his home, Tibet. There was only an endless line of white peaks under the blue sky. But he knew that crossing the border was a fateful step; his life would never be the same again. It seemed so long ago that Pasang had promised him an adventure. He'd never realized what that would really mean.

Suddenly Pasang gripped his shoulder, and again Tenzin froze. Around them, the others had stopped also.

"Look, on the other side of the cairn. There's something else—someone else."

Against the snow, Tenzin could see dark shapes moving in the distance, human shapes. It was a little group, crouched or leaning over something shaped like a triangle.

A wave of alarm ran through their group. Was that a mounted machine gun? It was too far away to tell.

"Go back—it's a trap!" someone shouted.

Tenzin turned to run, anticipating the gunfire that was about to erupt. But Pasang stopped him. "Wait," he said. Their guide was striding toward the strangers. He didn't seem afraid. There were smiles and lots of nodding.

"Aren't they border guards?" Tenzin asked. Pasang was too engrossed in the scene to answer.

A few moments later, the guide was returning, the strangers with him. They wore lots of clothes and big boots, and they carried large bags on their backs and cameras slung around their necks. One reminded Tenzin of their own guide, with his ruddy-brown, lined face, dressed like a Sherpa for the mountains. The others looked like nothing Tenzin had ever seen before. One was tall and rangy, with pale skin and a shaggy beard. *Like people, but from another world,* he thought.

"It's all right," the guide said. "They're harmless."

Tenzin could feel a wave of relief flow through the group around him. A few were even shaking hands with the strange men. But others stayed wary, keeping their distance. Tenzin was still dazed by the shock of seeing other people on the mountain. He realized now how alone they had been.

The encounter had no effect on the plans of their guide, who wanted to keep moving. "It's getting cold, and we need to lose altitude as soon as we can." The group abruptly parted from the strangers, and Tenzin soon lost sight of them.

"Not long from now, you will be in Kathmandu, the capital of Nepal," their guide announced confidently. "There you can claim the protection of the Office of the Dalai Lama. They have a refugee center in the city, with food and warm clothes."

Tenzin beamed. But nearby, Sonam grunted and looked skeptical. "We still have a long way to go before we reach Kathmandu," he said aside to Pasang and Tenzin. He guessed it was another two hundred miles. "And just because we've left Chinese territory, it doesn't mean we're out of danger.

"Monks from my monastery have taken this route," he warned. "Snowstorms come upon travelers suddenly here, and crevasses give way without warning. But worse are the Nepali gangs. I have heard that refugees have been stripped of everything valuable by robbers, and left to die on the Death Pass."

That night they kept walking, stopping for ten minutes every hour or so. The exhilaration Tenzin had felt at the border was short-lived. Soon he was more concerned about the urgent pain in his feet. When the group stopped, he took off his shoes and rubbed his feet to bring the feeling back. He looked in alarm at the white patches he found on his skin. He tore off the patches, but felt no pain. Then he knew: the early stages of frostbite had set in. He said nothing to Pasang when it was time to move on; he must not slow them down anymore.

By early morning, with the temperature at its lowest, Tenzin's head was covered with frozen snow. He remembered with yearning the sheepskin coats his mother made for the family to wear in winter, and clutched his blanket more tightly around him. But when the sun rose, things got worse.

Tenzin's eyes felt gritty and were swollen shut. He rubbed them to ease the pain, but it did no good. When he forced them open, the mountains moved in and out of focus, and the sky looked dark. He peered around for Pasang, or Pema, but he couldn't recognize the hazy forms of people around him. He had no idea what was happening.

"Pasang, help me," he cried, terrified. "I can't see!"

Instantly Pasang was at his side. He examined Tenzin's eyes, bloodshot and full of tears. He called the guide over, and the grizzled man peered at Tenzin's swollen eyes for a moment before pulling Pasang aside and talking urgently to him.

When Pasang returned, he took Tenzin by the hand.

"Tenzin, listen to me. You're going to be fine. Up here, the sun reflects off the white snow and it can burn your eyes. You've got something called snow blindness. It will wear off. Here, I'll try something."

Pasang took out a piece of cloth and put it over Tenzin's eyes, and blew gently through it.

"I think that's better. I'm sure it is," Tenzin whimpered.

But his vision grew worse, and Pasang had to lead him by the hand all day. When the sun set Tenzin sobbed with fear; in the dark he could see nothing at all. During the night he left the path to pee, and couldn't find his way back.

"Pasang!" he howled at the top of his voice. Moments passed, agonizingly long. Tenzin could hear nothing but the wind. Had they left him behind?

When he heard Pasang's voice, he cried with relief. He clung to his brother's strong hand, leading him back to the others. Tenzin continued to hold tight, still shaking with sobs. At last Pasang pulled his hand away.

"Pasang," Tenzin pleaded.

"What have I done?" Pasang moaned quietly, as if he were talking to himself. "I should never have brought you."

Tenzin shuddered. "Don't say that, Pasang!"

"It's true," he snapped. "From the beginning I had doubts, whenever you cried or complained, but I kept going. I thought I could protect you, even keep you from knowing how dangerous this is. Now I know it was a mistake. As soon as I learned we were climbing up to the Death Pass, I started to realize how terrible a mistake I'd made. And I've been carrying everything for us—the straps on my pack have been biting into my shoulders, drawing blood. And you never stop: 'I'm cold, I'm hungry'—always hungry!"

"Pasang, I won't complain anymore!"

Pasang didn't seem to be listening. "I knew the guide was lying when he said we were close to Kathmandu, even before Sonam said anything."

They walked in silence for a while.

"There's nothing we can do about it now," Pasang sighed. "The fact is, it's more dangerous now to go back than to go forward."

Tenzin rubbed his sore eyes; they were dry now. Pasang's bitter words had shaken him out of his tears. But did Pasang really wish he'd left him behind? Maybe he was just angry now. Tenzin wanted desperately to be brave, to show Pasang he could be. But with his dimming sight, he felt he had entered a terrible, bleak place, cut off and alone. And he was afraid that he would never see again.

➤

The next day, they began the trek down the mountain. The cruel wind was weakening, and in the daylight Tenzin could at least see something, though the blue sky looked black. As he walked, he could make out only white and shades of gray.

With the border far behind them, the group decided to stop for a whole night to recover their strength. Sonam and Rinchen found enough yak dung and twigs to light a fire. Food was brought out and shared; hot tea and porridge were made and hungrily eaten. While Pasang fanned the fire with a yak-skin bellows, Tenzin settled down to rest. Sitting a little apart from the others, Tsering was praying loudly, the familiar drone of his voice a sound Tenzin had learned to ignore. Tenzin squinted at the blurred form of his brother, hoping for a sign that everything was all right again. He had spoken very little to Tenzin all day. But Pasang was looking east, at the view of Mount Everest. The others were also gazing tiredly at the highest place in the world.

"Look at all the snow on Chomalongma," Sonam mused.

Pema looked back at him. "We don't have to climb up there, do we? So let's forget about it."

Pasang chuckled. At last he turned to Tenzin. "Get some sleep," he said.

That night Tenzin dreamed in bright colors. He saw the brilliant green of the grass on the hills around his village, the crops of yellow barley in the fields, the brown of the mud-brick walls—even the vivid plumage of the wild pheasants that roosted nearby. When he awoke, he saw only the dark shadows of the desolate Snow Mountains, and he was aware of nothing but the intense cold, and the pain in his eyes. But he was determined not to complain. *I've got to show Pasang he wasn't wrong to bring me,* he reminded himself.

But Pasang had alarming news for him. While they were sleeping, their guide had disappeared.

CHAPTER 8

A Shout in the Dark

It was a bitter blow. Their leader had returned over the pass to Tibet to meet another group of refugees, leaving them to find their own way down to Kathmandu. All around Tenzin, the panicked refugees were reeling from the news. Who would take charge and make decisions for them now?

"We can find our own way," Pasang said quickly.

But Tenzin could hear nervousness in Pasang's voice, even if he couldn't see his brother's face clearly. They were leaderless and vulnerable, in danger of arrest by local police, easy prey to robbers. If they lost their way, there were physical perils. Winding down steep valleys on narrow paths, they could easily slip and fall to their deaths.

Once they were under way, Pasang leaned close to Tenzin and spoke quietly. "Listen, yesterday the guide warned us that the government in Nepal is under pressure from China to send fugitives back to Tibet. Until we register as refugees, we could be arrested and handed back to the Chinese. So stay near me," he added.

Tenzin didn't need the warning. Every instinct told him to shadow Pasang more closely than ever.

➤

Tenzin began to notice that something had changed: the snow was melting under his feet. Here and there he even spotted exposed grass and solid rock. They were now below the snow line, in the inhabited area of Nepal. The paths became easier to follow, and they came across other travelers, local Nepali people dressed in warm woolen clothing on their way between villages. Some led yaks as pack animals, but most carried their burdens of food or firewood in woven wicker baskets tied on their backs. The Nepalis ignored the ragged group of Tibetans, walking past them without even a word of greeting.

They pressed onward, skirting round the villages to avoid Nepali police. As they encountered more and more people, Tenzin could sense the group around him getting nervous.

Pasang seemed to sense it too. "Look," he proposed to everyone when they had paused for a rest, "I think it's safest if we rest during the day and walk through the night." He looked around. "Agreed?"

Everyone nodded.

Pasang searched for a hidden spot off the path, where they could sleep in the shadows, leaning against the rocks. They lay within earshot of a village, and Tenzin was kept awake by howling dogs and the cries of children, but not for long. It seemed too soon when Pasang shook him awake.

"Get up. We're setting off now."

The peaks of the high mountains were ghostly white in the moonlight. The group gathered up their belongings and started to walk. In the darkest hours of the night, Tenzin struggled to stay awake on his feet. He clung to Pasang's arm as he groped drowsily ahead, nearly blind in the dark. He could hear the sound of rushing water far below him.

"Everyone, stop!" Pasang's shout startled him. Tenzin pressed himself against the rocky wall next to his shoulder and stood still. He could hear Pema breathing behind him.

"We've missed the path in the dark," his brother said.

Tenzin listened to the torrent of water below. "Where are we?" he gasped.

"We're on a cliffside, above a river—that's all I know."

Leading Tenzin by the hand, Pasang inched carefully forward. A commotion behind Tenzin made them stop again. A scrabbling noise, like loose stones falling, and a loud yell pierced the night.

The shouting stopped suddenly. Next to Tenzin, Pema stood frozen, her silhouette a sharp outline in the moonlight. The only sound was the distant roar of the river.

"Tsering's fallen!" It was the voice of Sonam's cousin, Rinchen. "The old man must be dead," he called. "Either the fall or the river must have killed him."

No one moved. "We have to *do* something," Pema whispered.

Pasang took a deep breath. He leaned in closer to Tenzin. "You wait here with Pema," he said. "Don't move!" He dropped Tenzin's hand and felt his way across to Rinchen. "Let's see if we can find him down there," he called.

Tenzin waited as Pasang and Rinchen carefully climbed down the scree.

"Listen," he heard Rinchen say from a distance, "I hear moaning."

Long moments passed while Tenzin remained frozen, tense against the rocky ledge. Then Rinchen shouted up to them.

"We've found him! He's all right, but he's hurt."

Pasang and Rinchen pulled Tsering back up the cliffside. He was injured, but conscious, his head bleeding from a gash. Rinchen tore up some cloth to make a bandage.

"He was lucky. A boulder blocked his fall into the river," Pasang explained. Then he turned to Tenzin. "One wrong step can cost you your life," he said fiercely. "Stay very close, right?"

For the next few hours, they moved carefully ahead, watching each other constantly. As dawn approached, Pasang again took on the task of searching for a place to rest. This time he discovered a barn full of sheep, warm and protected. At home Tenzin was used to having the livestock around the house during the winter. But they were kept in their own separate room.

"I can't stand the smell," he said in disgust. "The sheep are peeing everywhere, and they step on you." Instantly, he regretted complaining.

But Pasang was too tired to get angry. "I know it's hard, but we have no choice. At least it's warm."

Tenzin tossed and turned, trying to ignore the stench. Lying awake, he suddenly noticed that his eyes did not hurt so much. Then he remembered how Pema had stood out against the moonlight on the cliffside.

"Pasang, I just realized something!" he whispered.

"Hmmm," Pasang answered sleepily.

"When we were walking tonight, I could see! I mean, much better than I have for a long time."

"That's good," Pasang said, but he sounded only half awake. Then Tenzin felt the pressure of his brother's hand on his shoulder. He reached up to hold it, and almost immediately fell asleep.

➤

Descending farther into the green and fertile valleys of Nepal, Tenzin stared in wonder at the food that grew around him. There were banana plants, apple orchards, hazelnut and walnut trees. It reminded Tenzin of the fruit from his grandmother's orchard, sweet apricots and plums. Here there was plenty of food, but he was starving. By the side of the path, they found wild strawberries to eat. Pasang stopped to pull up some corncobs that Nepali farmers had planted close to the path. He saw Tenzin watching him.

"We have to steal," he explained simply, "or we won't survive."

"Can't we buy something to eat?"

"We have no money left," Pasang said, lowering his voice. "And no one in the group is going to lend us any. They haven't got very much, and if they lend it to us, they know they'll never get it back."

Lagging behind the others, Pasang and Tenzin passed a Nepali family having a midday meal in their front yard. Tenzin stopped in his tracks and inhaled the delicious smell of rice and *dhal*, the tasty curry dish made with lentils. He looked pleadingly at the mother. At last she took pity on them both and gave them some leftovers. Tenzin almost cried with gratitude. They ate quickly, and hurried to catch up.

In his halting Tibetan, Tenzin told Pema how good the rice and *dhal* had tasted.

"Look over there," said Pema, pointing. "There are bananas on that tree. Come on, let's pick some."

With her friend Dawa, they climbed into the orchard and picked some bananas. Tenzin peeled one and bit into it, then made a face. It was green and unripe, and tasted like wood.

"We'll have to cook them," laughed Dawa.

When Pasang saw him, he warned him not to do it again.

"Watch out for the farmers, Tenzin. If they catch you, they'll beat you, and maybe hand you over to the police. Then we'll never get to India."

"But they looked so good," pleaded Tenzin.

"Just be careful."

They walked on until they came to a fork in the path. In the lead, Pasang paused, looking unsure as to which direction to take.

"Let's rest here until someone passes by," he said. "I learned some English in India. I'm sure some of the people around here speak it. I can ask for directions."

Soon a man approached. As he stopped, there was much fluttering and squawking behind him. The noise came from the wicker basket he carried on his back, full of live chickens.

"*Namaste,*" Pasang began, using the traditional Nepalese greeting. But the smattering of English he offered afterwards was met with a blank face. Pasang used sign language to ask him the way to Kathmandu, but the man kept walking. Pasang stopped other locals, but they all shook their heads.

"I bet the people up here have no idea where Kathmandu is!" he said, kicking at the dirt in exasperation. Tenzin watched him as he looked up one path, then the other.

"Come on, this way," he said decisively at last. The others followed.

Pema fell into step with Pasang. "I'm glad you're here," she said once they were under way. "Everyone's relying on you now." Pasang laughed, but look flustered.

Tenzin trailed behind them, listening. He noticed his brother laughed more often when Pema was around. A little later, he tugged his brother's shirt.

"Pasang, do monks get married?"

"No," his brother answered absently. Tenzin thought for a while.

"Pasang, are you still going to be a monk?"

Pasang looked surprised. Then he smiled and shrugged. "Who knows?" he said. Tenzin wasn't sure if he was teasing or not.

CHAPTER 9

Tenzin's Nightmare

Cloud crept up the valley, as it did at the end of every afternoon. Night was approaching as Pasang led the way farther down the mountain toward a river.

At the bottom of the slope, he slowed his pace before a narrow metal suspension bridge. Suddenly Pasang froze, and the others halted behind him. Tenzin peeked around his brother. At the end of the bridge was a police post. Inside he could see a man in uniform, smoking a cigarette. It was getting dark and murky; perhaps he hadn't seen them.

"Keep down!" Pasang whispered to the group.

They shuffled back along the track, and hid behind a wall. Pasang crept forward to get another look at the policeman. Tenzin waited fearfully for his return.

"He hasn't moved," Pasang reported when he had crawled back. "But we'll have to stay here until night. Maybe we can get across then."

Tenzin took the opportunity to snatch some sleep. A few hours later, Pasang woke his brother and the others.

"Stay here. I'll go ahead check it out."

Tenzin watched as Pasang moved silently across the metal bridge, taking care not to make it rattle, toward the police post. He returned and waved them forward. "It's empty," he whispered.

The group walked gingerly over the bridge. Farther down the valley, by some ruined houses, they faced a crossroads.

Pasang looked doubtfully up each path. "Let's go sleep behind those old walls," he said. "Tomorrow morning we'll find someone who knows the way."

They hid themselves, nestling alongside the decrepit walls. *At least it's warm here,* Tenzin thought. He was exhausted, and sleep came quickly.

In his dreams that night, Tenzin stood in a barley field. The sun was so bright he had to put his hands in front of his face to protect his eyes. There was no sound—no wind, no birds, just dead silence. He opened his fingers and saw a woman. She was scything the corn with rhythmic movements, sweeping back and forth. She turned toward him. And Tenzin realized with a shock that it was his mother. He tried to cry out to her. She mouthed something to him, but he heard nothing. He found that he was unable to move. He felt very frightened.

His mother came toward him, and then he heard her speak, very distinctly.

Tenzin woke suddenly, gasping for breath, his chest heaving. He quickly remembered where he was, and that Pasang was lying next to him. But his mind was still filled with the disturbing dream. And he remembered the words his mother had spoken.

"Be strong," she had said. "And be prepared for the worst." Then he had known that something awful was going to happen very soon.

Tenzin had no idea what the awful thing might be. But possibilities crowded his mind. The first, which made his heart pound, was losing Pasang. Or what if they were arrested and sent back? Or if he or Pasang got sick and couldn't go on? He lay still with his eyes closed, breathing slowly to calm himself.

It was just a dream, thought Tenzin.

He would keep his fears to himself, and not bother Pasang about a dream. But the bad feeling in the pit of his stomach persisted. He slept fitfully for the rest of the night.

➤

At dawn Tenzin awoke to see a young girl standing over them. She wore a colorful headscarf, and was holding schoolbooks.

Next to him, Pasang scrambled to his feet, as the girl stepped back. He gestured in sign language, asking, "Kathmandu?" The girl smiled. Cheerfully, she turned and pointed the way down the valley. Pasang thanked her excitedly. He turned to Tenzin, his face beaming.

"Ha!" he said. "We get nothing but blank stares all day when we ask for directions, and then help comes while we're lying asleep!" Tenzin hadn't seen Pasang look so happy in a long time.

Together they roused the others. As they set off again, Tenzin tried to forget his dream, and said nothing about it. He noticed Pasang was looking quizzically at him.

"What is it?" Tenzin asked.

"Your face, it's very red," Pasang said.

Tenzin touched his cheek, which he now realized was feeling itchy.

"Maybe it's the heat," Pasang added quickly, and picked up his pace.

The wintry conditions of the Snow Mountains were far behind; now Tenzin could feel the tropical heat of the lowlands in Nepal. The air was close and oppressive. Sonam and Rinchen stopped at a market to buy new shoes to replace the ones they'd worn out on the mountains. Tenzin watched dejectedly.

"We've no money," Pasang reminded him, "so we'll have to make do with what we've got."

Tenzin looked down at his torn sneakers, disintegrating under his feet. And now the skin on his face and chest was very itchy. He thought again about his dream. Was this what it meant—was he ill? Should he tell Pasang? His feeling of foreboding returned.

"What's wrong now?" Pasang said, watching him.

"I thought that once we crossed the mountains the rest would be easy," Tenzin tried to explain, but he knew he sounded sulky. "You never told me the whole way to India was going to be so hard."

Sonam and Rinchen had finished their purchases, and Pasang started walking again, saying nothing.

"It's just not what I expected at all," Tenzin said, then bit his lip. He'd done it again; he'd complained.

But Pasang looked deep in thought. After a while he seemed to have made a decision. He turned to Tenzin.

"However much we suffer now, it's nothing compared to

what Mother went through. Did she tell you what happened during the bad times, the Great Leap Forward and the so-called Cultural Revolution?"

"No," said Tenzin. "She never talked about it."

"She never told me about it either, until those few months ago when I came back. It's a terrifying story. I think she wanted to spare you, and it was too painful for her to talk about it. It's only because she's so strong that she survived."

Tenzin thought of how little his mother used to talk about her past, and how she had seemed to hold something back, some secret that he was afraid to ask about. He felt afraid to hear it now, too.

But Pasang went on. "During those times," he explained, "Mao Zedong, the Chinese leader who ordered the invasion of Tibet, sent in Red Guards to impose Communism on the country. They smashed up the monasteries, tortured and killed monks and nuns, and tried to destroy the Tibetan way of life. Not just the leaders, but the ordinary people suffered greatly. That was while Mother was growing up.

"The family had nothing to eat. Everything they grew was sent away to China. So they went into the mountains, foraging. They dug up the roots of plants, chopped them up, and made a broth. They threw everything that was green into a big cauldron, boiled-up stalks, weeds, anything, because all the grain was collected by the government and sent away. If the Red Guards saw smoke from your chimney they suspected that you were keeping food back and they would arrive on your doorstep to denounce you.

"Mother told me that everyone in the village was allowed to eat just one spoonful of broth. It tasted disgusting, but it was all they had. Two men in the village thought they could find some grains down a rat hole, and scrabbled around in the dirt. They ate what they found there because they were so hungry. They both died. They had eaten dirt infected by the rats. Mother said that many people in the village starved to death."

Tenzin was very quiet. However hungry he had been at home, it had never been that bad.

"Then the government moved Mother's family away to another province to work in some potato fields. There was our mother, her six brothers and sisters, and our grandparents. They didn't have enough clothing, and no cloth to make any. Some of them had no trousers or shoes. 'They got so thin,' Mother said, 'that their legs and arms looked like sticks.' Four of the children died.

"Yes," Pasang said, seeing Tenzin's surprise, "they were four uncles and aunts we never met, we never even knew about." His eyes were flashing now, and Tenzin could hear the familiar anger growing in his voice. "Two of them died of starvation, two of some disease they caught because they were so weak. We had a great-uncle there, an old man. One day he fell ill and couldn't work in the fields. The Red Guards battered him to death. The same Red Guards beat some other people and buried them alive."

Pasang stopped suddenly and looked for a while back at the mountains, toward their homeland.

"There's something else she told me," he said, his voice calmer. "When the family was forced to leave the village, they took everything they could from the house—pots, pans, bits of furniture. The Red Guards ordered everyone to kill their pets, but the family couldn't bring themselves to kill their dog.

So the dog followed them. When they came to a large river, they had to swim across it. They had to leave most of their belongings behind. Our grandfather tied the dog to a post, and they crossed the river without him.

"Mother remembers that the dog barked and barked, and she cried because she couldn't bear the sound." He looked down at Tenzin. "But do you know what? Three years later, when they were able to go back home, the dog was waiting on the bank of that river. People around there told them that he had got loose and had been living in a cave waiting for them to return. Mother cried when she told me this."

They walked on, Tenzin silent and thoughtful. He turned the story over and over in his mind. It was the stuff of nightmares, and he knew it would haunt him for a long time to come. *I'll never complain again,* he vowed. He would make Pasang, and his mother, proud of him. And he said nothing about his dream.

CHAPTER 10

Among the Palaces
of Kathmandu

Exhausted and footsore, Tenzin and Pasang staggered into
Nepal's steamy central valley. Four weeks had passed since
the truck had dropped them off in the foothills of the Snow
Mountains to begin their climb. Physically, the toughest part
of their ordeal was behind them. Another kind of challenge
lay ahead.

Among the orange groves and rice fields, the ragged
band of Tibetans threaded their way past ornate buildings,
Hindu temples, and holy shrines. Tenzin stared at them
all in wonder. Soon the temples and shrines became more
numerous; they were nearing the great city of Kathmandu.
Pasang looked watchful, his eyes wary. Tenzin had no idea
what to expect, but he braced himself for his first glimpse of
this strange and wonderful place.

As they entered the city, the fumes, the stink of open
drains, and the great throng of humanity nearly overwhelmed

him. Their goal was Boudnath, a suburb where many exiled Tibetans lived.

"That's where we'll find the refugee center. We'll be safe there," Pasang explained.

He led Tenzin through the narrow streets, past the ancient carved wooden balconies of the houses. The city squares were built around palaces, temples, and monuments as grand as anything in Lhasa except for the Potala Palace. But Tenzin stared most of all at the markets. There were stalls full of ripe fruit and fresh vegetables; he saw fish and meat for sale. It made his mouth water.

"Look!" said Pasang. "There are Tibetans here."

Pema and Dawa cheered, and everyone looked encouraged; it meant that they were approaching Boudnath.

Soon Boudnath's great *stupa* came into view. The domed Buddhist monument, one of the largest of its kind in the world, soared overhead. Honoring Buddha, it was a site of pilgrimage and meditation. Rising above its dome was a tall central pillar, and on each of its four sides a pair of eyes was painted—the vast all-seeing eyes of Buddha the Compassionate One, looking out across the valley to all four points of the compass. Tenzin was awestruck. Brass prayer-wheels were built into the base of the sacred *stupa*, and Tenzin watched as Tsering set them spinning, praying loudly to the Buddha. Even as he prayed, Tsering looked slyly at the crowds moving about them.

Pasang nudged Tenzin. "He's always looking for a chance to beg."

Together the brothers made the expected prayer-walk clockwise around the domed *stupa*, in honor of the Buddha.

But even though they were surrounded by their own people, Pasang and Tenzin and their group stood out from the other Tibetans. They were clearly refugees: weather-beaten, dirty, and bedraggled.

"You must be careful," a local shopkeeper warned Pasang. "It's obvious you're newcomers. Your clothes and baggage give you away. Get off the streets, or the police will arrest you."

"He's right," Pasang said to the others. "We have to get to the refugee center now. And it would be safer if we split up and met there."

Breaking off into groups of two or three, they moved warily through the city, crossing the busy Kathmandu Ring Road. Finally they met up again in the courtyard of the Refugee Reception Center, a single-story building at the foot of a tall hill topped by a temple.

"We'll be safe here from the police," Pasang reassured Tenzin. "And from thieves who know we have no right to be in the country," he added.

An official met them at the door, as if he'd been expecting them. He led them into an office, where he motioned for them to sit down on benches against the wall. Then he left them. Tenzin sat close to Pasang, staring up at a whirring electric fan.

A man in a dark jacket and a flat cloth hat entered the room and sat at the metal desk. He introduced himself as the Director of the Refugee Center.

He spoke to them at length. At first Tenzin tried to follow his words, but he was not speaking Tenzin's dialect, and he talked too quickly for Tenzin to follow his Tibetan. Tenzin saw Pasang and Pema smile at each other at what the man said, and Sonam and his cousin grunted their approval. That was a good sign. Tenzin sat back and waited for Pasang to translate for him.

Suddenly he saw Pasang's smile fade. What had the man just said?

But then the Director stood up, and used a Tibetan word Tenzin knew well: "*Za.*" It meant "Eat"! Tenzin sat up eagerly. The Director beckoned to the group and led them through a nearby barley field to a barn. There were tables inside, and low beds. This was where they would stay.

Two women were cooking over paraffin stoves. Tenzin was given a plate of *dhal bhat*, the Nepalese dish of lentil soup and rice, which he ate voraciously. Next to him, Pasang squatted with his own meal. Between mouthfuls, he instructed Tenzin about what to do next.

"They can help us here. A man from the United Nations will come tomorrow and interview each of us. He's a very important man. We have to tell him why we left Tibet, how we suffered there, the hardships of our journey, our plans for the future. And why we can't go back. He'll listen, then make a decision. If he awards us official refugee status, we'll get a permit and some money, and we can continue our journey to India, and see the Dalai Lama."

Tenzin nodded as he shoveled more food into his mouth.

"But we have to be very careful what we say," Pasang added, leaning closer and lowering his voice. "If he doesn't believe us, we'll fail the interview."

"And then what?"

"Then we'll have to go back, over the Snow Mountains."

Tenzin nearly dropped his plate. Once again his dream, and his mother's warning, filled his mind. Despite the warm air, he shivered.

"So you must have your story ready. You must say that you want to study and learn about our language and religion. Then everything will be okay."

At that moment Tenzin did not care about his religion, or anything besides filling his empty belly and never having to see the Snow Mountains again. But he nodded to show he understood.

That evening they settled down to sleep in the dormitory. Sitting on his metal bunk, Tenzin bounced a little, as if to make sure it was really true—he was going to sleep in a bed tonight. Next to him, Pasang took out a small package that he had kept hidden in the depths of his backpack.

"Now I can tell you more about the Dalai Lama," Pasang said, his voice low and solemn. "It's safe here." He showed Tenzin his photograph of the holy man, dressed in monk's robes. Tenzin leaned closer and looked at the image his brother had shown him once before, so briefly, when he had come home. This time he felt as if someone had offered to open the door to a secret room, long locked and forbidden.

"Remember the Potala Palace in Lhasa? That's where the Dalai Lamas lived for hundreds of years. 'Dalai Lama' means 'Ocean of Wisdom' in the Mongolian language. And this Dalai Lama, the fourteenth, was born near our village. When he was a little boy, he was recognized as the reincarnation of the Thirteenth Dalai Lama, who had died a few years before. He was taken to live in the Potala Palace, but when the Chinese invaded Tibet, he was forced into exile. To escape, he disguised himself and climbed over the Snow Mountains, just like us. He took a route farther to the east beyond a kingdom called Bhutan, and went to India.

The Indians let him stay. He and others who followed him set up a new Tibetan government there, a government-in-exile. And tomorrow we'll be granted our passes, and we'll be able to travel to India, and see him there."

Tenzin took the photograph from his brother and held it gently. He looked more closely at the monk with the kind smile, the same face he had seen in his mother's picture under the bed.

"Why didn't you tell me all this before?"

"I didn't want you to know more than you needed to," Pasang said. "Just in case we were captured, and you were interrogated. If you say anything about our leader-in-exile, anything at all, the Chinese guards beat you."

Pasang smiled. "But now that we are in Nepal, we can talk about the Dalai Lama all we want."

That night Tenzin slept soundly in his bunk, needing no blankets in the heat of the Kathmandu valley. But the next morning, he awoke feeling uneasy. He could not stop thinking about his dream.

Nearby, Sonam caught his attention. He was pulling something out of his backpack with a flourish. With obvious pride, Sonam put on the red robes he had carried over the Himalayas. "It's safe now to be a monk!" he announced.

Together the group returned across the barley field to the refugee center. It was time to be registered, their first step toward achieving official refugee status. For the next few hours, Tenzin and Pasang were called from room to room, and pushed through a complicated and bewildering procedure. Passport-size photographs were taken, personal information entered into a large ledger, and signatures obtained. Tenzin signed his name in Chinese, the only language he knew how to write. He watched Tsering take his turn next, bending over the book and signing with a cross.

He can't write his own name, Tenzin realized. Then he noticed Tsering was wearing glasses. Tenzin had never seen him do that before.

"Why is he wearing glasses?" Tenzin whispered to Pasang.

His brother suppressed a laugh. "He says they make him look more important," he whispered back.

"Where did he get them?"

"He must have stolen them from somebody."

In the afternoon, a nurse examined each of them. She looked at Tenzin's face and chest.

"Your brother is suffering from scabies," she told Pasang. "It's a skin infection caused by tiny mites," she added, seeing his puzzled expression. She gave him some ointment. Pasang told her about the snow blindness, and the nurse examined Tenzin's eyes. Tenzin sat very still and waited, his heart beating fast.

She stepped back at last. "It will fade," she assured him. "There won't be any lasting effects."

Next she injected him with a vaccine to protect against tuberculosis. *The needle hurts,* Tenzin thought, *but it's better than walking over mountains.*

➤

In the afternoon, Tenzin, Pasang, and the others basked in the sun that warmed the center's courtyard. Pasang straightened as a car pulled up to the gate. Out of it stepped an imposing man in a dark suit. The Director of the Refugee Center rushed outside to greet him, removing his cloth cap in deference. He turned and addressed the small crowd in the courtyard.

"This is Mr. Aziz from the United Nations Refugee Agency," he announced solemnly. The scruffy group sprang to their feet and bowed.

"*He's* the very important man," Pasang whispered to his brother. "He signs the papers that allow us to go to India."

Tenzin swallowed. He followed the others inside and watched as, one by one, his companions were called into the office to be interviewed by Mr. Aziz through an interpreter. First Sonam, then Pema and Dawa emerged smiling, waving their official letters.

When Pasang's turn came, he squeezed Tenzin's shoulder and left him waiting nervously outside. After what seemed like an age, Pasang came out beaming. In his hand was a piece of paper. He showed it to Tenzin.

"See this? It says that I have Official Refugee Status, and I can travel to India. Now it's your turn."

Tenzin stood up to go. He turned back and looked questioningly at Pasang. His brother nodded encouragingly. Tenzin stepped into the office and sat on the metal chair in front of Mr. Aziz's desk. The interpreter, a woman in an Indian dress, asked Tenzin a question. But Tenzin didn't understand. Mr. Aziz pointed at Tenzin's passport-size photograph in the ledger, and showed it to Tenzin.

"Ah!" Tenzin realized they wanted to know his name. He tapped his chest. "Tenzin . . . Tenzin."

The woman continued to ask him questions, and seemed to be trying different languages, but Tenzin couldn't understand any of them. None of them was the dialect of northern Tibet that Tenzin and Pasang used. Questions were fired at him, but were nothing but meaningless noise. In a panic, Tenzin looked round for Pasang.

He'll be able to translate for me, he thought hopefully.

Through the office window he could see Pasang, looking agitated and concerned. Mr. Aziz and the interpreter were shaking their heads.

Mr. Aziz looked at Tenzin and pointed at the door. He was being ordered out of the office. Tenzin slid off his chair and walked out. He realized with a sudden pang that he had been given no paper.

There was a hurried conversation between Mr. Aziz and the Director of the Refugee Center, who came over to Pasang.

Tenzin watched them talk. He could tell Pasang was getting more agitated. His brother swallowed and closed his hands into fists as he listened. When he answered the Director, his voice was loud and indignant. The Director kept talking a little longer in a calm voice. Pasang looked stunned for a moment.

Suddenly he turned to Tenzin and grabbed his hand, dragging him outside into the courtyard where the others had gathered again. He sat miserably on a bench, pulling Tenzin down beside him.

Tenzin stared at him in alarm. "Pasang, what's wrong? What happened?"

"Mr. Aziz won't grant you refugee status. He doesn't believe you're Tibetan."

"What?"

"He thinks you may be Chinese or Mongolian. In the interview you couldn't answer any of his questions."

"You need to translate for me!"

"That's what I told him. I said we speak a dialect from the north. But he won't let me. The rules state that you have to be interviewed individually. No one can translate for you."

Tenzin gaped, horrified.

"The Director says we can stay here, but just for tonight. Without refugee status, you can't go on to India. And you can't stay in Nepal."

"What will we do?"

Pasang paused a moment and sighed heavily. "I'll have to take you back home to Tibet," he said finally, then buried his face in his hands.

Seeing Pasang's dismay, Pema and Dawa rushed over to the brothers.

"The United Nations are no help to us," Pasang complained to them. "They say we must be Mongolians. At one time in our history, the place where we live was in Mongolia, but now it's in Tibet. Others from the same place have been allowed to go to monasteries in India. I don't know what they're thinking, but they are not giving Tenzin a permit. They have told us to go back.

"Go back!" he shouted in outrage, his fists clenched. "I'm so angry, but what can I do? I'm helpless." He hung his head.

Pema and Dawa murmured their sympathy. Pasang frantically stroked his matted hair as he considered his options. "We have no money left to get out of here. Going back is unthinkable! But without the official papers it's no use for us. We can't go on."

"It's all my fault, isn't it?" Tenzin asked. Maybe it really had been a mistake to bring him, after all. He watched his brother for an answer, but Pasang refused to look at him. Pema put her hand over Tenzin's.

Tenzin barely noticed. He sat frozen, transfixed by the dread of what lay ahead. *So this is what the dream meant,* he thought. They were condemned to make the grueling journey back over the Snow Mountains. All their efforts, all the pain and fear he had felt, all the hardships they had endured, had been for nothing. Tenzin felt tears sting his eyes.

I have to stay strong, he reminded himself, *I must not cry.*

Tenzin squeezed his eyes shut and tried to think of something to stop the flow of tears. He pictured his friend Sangye, and the day they went fishing, before all this had started. He focused his mind on the river. It was full of fish, glittering in the sun, and he was trying to catch them. But try as he might, he couldn't catch any. They just slipped through his fingers.

CHAPTER 11

Pasang's Gamble

Pasang lay on his bunk, while Tenzin perched at the end of the bed, listening to his brother weigh their options, calculating the risks.

"Going home has its own dangers," Pasang mused aloud. "It's not just admitting we failed. It's going to take a huge effort to climb back over the Snow Mountains. I just don't know if we have the strength for that now."

He and Tenzin had come a long way, over 1,500 miles, from their village. In contrast, their goal was tantalizingly close. From Kathmandu it was less than 100 miles to the border with India. But how could they continue their journey without official papers? Should they try to sneak over the border? They would most likely be caught.

"And even if we manage to reach my monastery in India," Pasang continued, "it could end up being for nothing. Tibetan monasteries in India are forbidden to shelter illegal refugees. By law, they'd have to turn us over for deportation anyway."

Pasang rose and wandered restlessly in the dormitory. Tenzin followed, afraid to lose sight of him. No one was sleeping yet. Tenzin looked around at the people he had come to know in the mountains; in this strange place they seemed almost like old friends.

"Maybe we could use some advice," Pasang said.

Sonam and Rinchen listened intently to Pasang. Tenzin's plight seemed to rouse Sonam's love of desperate causes. "We'll help any way we can," he declared immediately, his eyes lighting up. Meanwhile Pema and Dawa had joined them, sitting on either side of Tenzin like protective mother hens.

"You must get through somehow. There has to be a way," said Pema. "Dawa and I have been talking. We can share the money they gave us here. It'll be enough to buy bus tickets to India for all of us."

Pasang muttered his thanks. He looked too moved to say any more. Tenzin was surprised. He had expected that, whatever they decided to do, he and Pasang would carry on alone. He felt a little less hopeless now.

By morning Pasang had made up his mind.

"We're going to stay with the others," he told Tenzin, his face resolute, "and make the journey to India—without refugee status for you. I'm hoping that, somehow, if we stay together, the others will shield us from being discovered.

"I have to warn you, though, it's risky. If the police arrest us, we'll go to prison, then be deported. Do you understand?"

Tenzin nodded. If Pasang had hope, then so did he.

When the refugees left on the evening bus for Delhi, the brothers were among them.

➤

Six hours later, in the dead of night, the bus reached the Nepal–India border. Tenzin felt a rising sense of panic. He had been so happy to be on the bus that he hadn't yet thought about what would happen when they actually reached the border.

"We have to show our papers," Pema whispered to Pasang. "Quick, hide Tenzin."

Tenzin was glad Pema had insisted they sit at the back; now the other passengers wouldn't see what they were doing. Pasang bundled Tenzin under the seat, covering him with a coat. Sonam and Rinchen shuffled along their seats to help hide the stowaway.

"Pretend to be asleep," Tenzin heard Pema whisper to the others.

The Indian police boarded. Peeking out from under the coat, Tenzin watched them stride down the center aisle of the bus. They moved row by row, questioning passengers. Under the seat, Tenzin kept very still, his every muscle tensed. He listened for his own breathing, careful to make no sound.

One of the guards drew nearer; Tenzin closed his eyes and prayed. When he opened them, he saw Pema, one row ahead, smiling sweetly at the guard as she handed him a small wad of rupees. The man took the money and paused. Tenzin watched and waited. Shrugging his shoulders, the guard turned away without examining any of their papers.

When the guards got off and the bus was allowed to drive away, Tenzin climbed out and grinned at Pema as he took his place next to his brother.

"So far, so good," said Pasang, patting his back. They would continue their journey for now, onward to the Indian capital, where Tenzin faced an uncertain future as an illegal refugee.

➤

Tenzin felt a nudge in his ribs. He woke up, startled. His brother was smiling at him.

"Hey, Tenzin. The sun's coming up. Welcome to India."

Tenzin looked out the bus window at the countryside. It was as busy as a city—everywhere there were fields filled with people working continuously, like colonies of ants. He saw houses under construction, irrigation channels being dug, crops tended and animals herded, and market stalls where traders shouted. The teeming bustle of humanity was fascinating. The road itself was jammed with cars, buses, pedestrians, even cows on the loose.

As he watched, Tenzin realized to his delight that his eyesight had returned completely. What's more, his feet hurt less than they had in ages. He pulled off his shoes and examined them. Some skin was gone and there were still raw patches, but the blisters were healing. Tenzin put his shoes back on before anyone else saw his feet; he didn't want to add to Pasang's worries.

As the sun grew hotter, a new menace appeared on the bus: tiny, buzzing insects. Tenzin had never seen these creatures before. And they were attacking him!

"Mosquitoes," Sonam explained when he saw Tenzin's perplexed face.

Tenzin watched as they bit him. His flesh swelled up a little and started to itch. *Buddhists respect all living things,* he reminded himself, *so I must not kill them.* Out of compassion, he let them feed. Tenzin glanced up at his brother. Pasang was swatting the mosquitoes, his face annoyed.

Maybe I'm a better Buddhist than my brother, he thought with surprise.

As they entered the vast city of Delhi, India's capital, the air was warm and humid. Tenzin coughed as the exhaust fumes from thousands of cars leached into the bus. Here the traffic was chaotic, and the roads teemed with the largest crowds he had ever seen in his life. People were eating, sleeping, shouting, and even peeing in the street. Full of curiosity, Tenzin would have loved to explore the city. But he knew that he was not safe. Without that special paper all the others had, the Indian police could send him back to Tibet at any moment.

After a night at the center for Tibetan refugees in Delhi, the group boarded another bus. This time they were headed north, back into the foothills of the Himalayas to a town called Dharamsala.

"We're going to the home of the Dalai Lama," Pasang told Tenzin, "and the Tibetan government-in-exile."

Pema's face beamed with excited anticipation. But Tenzin was so tired that as soon as the bus's engine started up, he fell asleep.

➤

The bus drove on through the night, and by morning they were traveling through green forests in the clear, fresh air of the lower hills of the Himalayas. Above them soared high peaks, with snow on the upper slopes. Tenzin's heart leapt. The countryside looked so much like his homeland. The bus wound up steep mountain roads, narrowly avoiding the dangerous precipices on either side. *The driver must be very skillful,* Tenzin thought.

It was a bright October day when Pasang and Tenzin reached the chaotic bus station in Dharamsala. As the brothers stepped off, Tibetan faces swarmed all around them: red-robed monks, food sellers, a sea of people on the move. In the town there were familiar-looking Buddhist temples and monasteries, as well as hotels, shops, and cafés. And somewhere in all this bustle lived their leader, the Dalai Lama.

Pasang asked around for directions. "The Refugee Reception Center? Do you know where it is?"

They followed a friendly Tibetan dressed in a red cap and jacket, who led them past a succession of temples and prayer wheels. He pointed up some steps to a large building on the side of the hill.

Two large dormitories, one for men, the other for women, housed the continuous flow of new refugees. At least their travels were over for a day or two. Tenzin settled down on the bare floorboards next to Pasang and slept without interruption for twelve hours.

When they awoke, they were led to the kitchen and given tea and barley porridge. Back in the dormitory, the two brothers sorted out their meager belongings, washed themselves and some clothes, and found another cup of tea. Pasang rummaged about in his bag, and pulled something out.

"Let's have a look at these. My photographs."

They sat together as Pasang opened up the precious packet that he had carried with him on all his travels, never losing it to guards or thieves. He spread out the family photos, handing them to Tenzin one by one. Tenzin held them carefully, as if they were holy relics. There were pictures of their mother in happy times, Pasang as a young novice monk, the two of them together at home with their brothers. Some made Tenzin laugh; looking at others, he turned thoughtful.

Tenzin gazed at the picture of himself and Pasang in front of the Potala Palace in Lhasa. It seemed they had come a vast distance since then. He looked up at his brother.

"One day we'll show this one to Mother, won't we?" he said.

"I'm sure we will," Pasang replied confidently.

Later the same day, officials in the center checked in the new refugees. Again they were to be interviewed, and their papers scrutinized. Pasang and Tenzin filed with the others into the main office, where the staff eyed the newcomers warily. Each name was entered by hand in a large book. Tenzin stared at the hundreds of books on shelves lining the crowded office, the records of all the Tibetans who had passed through Dharamsala on their long journeys to freedom in exile.

Waiting for their turn was agonizing, as Tenzin braced himself for the ordeal of another interview. He noticed a commotion nearby; some of the staff were talking in agitated voices.

Pasang leaned over and whispered to Tenzin. "I just overheard something. There's talk that Chinese spies may have tried to infiltrate the Tibetan government-in-exile, and even breach the security around the Dalai Lama."

Tenzin looked at the suspicious, worried expressions on the faces of the officials. He just could imagine their reaction once they discovered he had no papers from Nepal!

When at last the brothers were summoned to the Director's office, Tenzin was relieved to find they would go in together. Tenzin had no idea what they would say; he knew only that this meeting was crucial. If all went well, this might be the day that he was granted his official papers. If not, he faced prison or deportation.

"I'll do the talking, all right?" Pasang whispered to him as they entered the room.

The Director of the Dharamsala Refugee Center sat behind a cluttered desk, reading through their documents. He looked harried, and beckoned impatiently for them to sit down. For some time he continued to examine Pasang's papers. Then he looked up at Tenzin.

"Why is there no pass from the United Nations for you, little one?" He jabbed a finger at him.

Tenzin glanced nervously at Pasang. He was pretty sure he'd understood the question, and with his small knowledge of Tibetan, he tried to piece together an answer. He took too long for the Director, who turned abruptly to Pasang.

"Did you go to Nepal?"

"Yes, we went through Nepal. I went home to get him."

The Director pointed at Tenzin. "Why wasn't he given an official letter in Nepal, like you?"

"Because he doesn't speak Tibetan, they thought he was Mongolian. He can't speak Mongolian or Chinese, but they just suspected he was." Pasang's words came out in a rush. The Director frowned.

"That's why they didn't give him a letter," Pasang concluded.

The official sighed, making it obvious that he was skeptical of Pasang's answers.

"You should have told them that he is not Chinese or Mongolian, and given reasons for it!"

"I told them that he's Tibetan," insisted Pasang.

"This is a very serious problem," the Director said sternly. "By our agreement with the Indian government, he is allowed to be in this country only if he has the appropriate papers. He will have to go back home."

Pasang leapt to his feet. "No, he is going to the monastery too!" he protested. "He wants to be a monk."

"Sit down!" ordered the Director. "It's not possible, because he hasn't got any official papers. It's all right for you, your papers are in order. You can go on to the monastery. But he can't."

The Director stopped addressing Pasang and wrote a brief report. He handed it over to Pasang.

"Take this letter and explain yourselves to the Office of His Holiness the Dalai Lama," he instructed tersely. "Do you want to take the boy with you to the monastery?"

"Yes, of course," Pasang said, his face bewildered. Tenzin was concentrating hard to follow the exchange, his eyes darting between Pasang and the Director.

Seeing their confusion, the official sighed and leaned forward on his desk.

"You have one chance left," he explained slowly. "You have to ask the Office of the Dalai Lama to help you. Do you understand?"

Pasang nodded.

"Tell them the truth." The Director emphasized each word. "Otherwise they will expel both of you. Tell the real story. Do you understand?"

He pointed to the letter Pasang held in his hands.

"I am passing your case on to the higher authority," he said, then shook his head before adding, "but you must prepare yourselves for your return to Tibet."

There was a pause. Tenzin looked questioningly at his brother, who stood still, holding the letter. He appeared drained, and close to despair. The Director glanced up at him with raised eyebrows when he made no move to leave.

"We're hungry," Pasang said quietly. "We have no money, nothing."

"I will tell the kitchen here to feed you for two days. Just two days, do you hear?"

With a curt nod, he dismissed them from the office. The brothers stepped out into the street.

"Pasang, what does it mean?" Tenzin asked, still confused by the outcome. "Do I have to go back?"

"Yes," Pasang said simply. "But I'll go back too. They don't understand our situation. And I can't go to the monastery without you. I made a promise to Mother, and now it looks as though I won't be able to keep it."

"But how do we go back? Can we get a bus?" Tenzin said hopefully.

"Yes, as far as the border. But we'll still have to walk back over the Snow Mountains."

Their gamble had failed. Pasang kept strolling dejectedly, but Tenzin stayed rooted where he stood, oblivious to the milling people who brushed past him. The tears he'd held back came now, running uncontrollably.

CHAPTER 12

In the Presence of the Living Buddha

"**J**ust tell them the truth," Sonam said passionately. "They can't send you back. It would be too cruel!"

Pema agreed. "Look at Tenzin. He's so small. There must be a way out of this."

Pasang listened and nodded, while Tenzin sat a little apart from their friends, his mind a whirlwind of uncertainties. He knew very little time remained for him and Pasang. They must either convince the "higher authority" the Director had spoken of, or return to Tibet.

He consoled himself with the news that in the meantime they would have a chance to see the Dalai Lama—if only at a distance. Sonam had discovered that "newcomers," refugees recently arrived from Tibet, were invited to a celebration. It was the anniversary of the founding of the school in Dharamsala known as the Tibetan Children's Village, and the Dalai Lama would be there.

The next day was brilliant with sunshine as the brothers made their way up the hill to the school, along with hundreds of other Tibetans. They found a spot to stand on a steep slope, facing the sports ground. Opposite them they could see a wooden throne under a sunshade, mounted on a platform, backed by a huge yellow, blue, and red Tibetan flag. This was where the exiled Tibetan leader would soon appear.

Suddenly all eyes turned to the entrance. Crowds parted in front of the Dalai Lama's Range Rover as it drove through the school gates in a cloud of dust. Pennants in the colors of the Tibetan flag fluttered above its headlights. Many in the crowd bowed their heads; some prostrated themselves on the ground. As the dust cleared, Tenzin stood on tiptoe to glimpse the Dalai Lama emerge, dressed in red robes. His head was shaved, and his face beamed in a serene smile.

He doesn't look so much like a god, Tenzin thought. *More like a lowly monk.*

The Dalai Lama bustled along a line of dignitaries, pressing his hands together in the posture of prayer, stooped in a humble way. All heads bobbed down as he passed, and many people kneeled. Tenzin felt sure there was an aura around this man, as though a special light were shining on him wherever he went.

After greeting rows of bowing schoolchildren, the Dalai Lama reached the podium and sat on the throne, indicating that everyone should also sit. Obediently, Pasang and Tenzin sat down cross-legged on the grass.

The Dalai Lama tapped the microphone and, satisfied that it was working, began to address his people. He spoke of long exile, and of the hope that lay in education and schools such as this one. Pasang listened carefully, translating whatever Tenzin could not understand. Tenzin gazed across the sea of people at the holy man. There, before his own eyes, was the Reincarnation of the Living Buddha of Compassion. Even from far away, Tenzin could see his earnest, good-natured face. *I'll bet if he heard our story,* Tenzin thought, *he'd understand.* But it seemed impossible that he could ever cross that distance to plead their cause.

➤

That night Tenzin tossed and turned. He was awoken early by a buzz of excitement in the dormitory.

Sonam's face appeared in the doorway. "Hurry, get ready," he called. "The Director just told us we have been granted an audience with His Holiness."

"When?" Pasang asked groggily.

"This morning—now! Come on."

Pasang turned to Tenzin. "I can hardly believe it," he said, amazed. "This is our chance! It's almost too good to be true. I've been waiting to ask the officials in the Dalai Lama's office for a decision, but this is so much better—don't you see? We're going to see *him,* the Dalai Lama, face to face!" Tenzin saw his brother's hand shaking as he tucked the Director's letter into his pocket.

Soon the brothers had joined the long line of refugees waiting in the courtyard of the Dalai Lama's official residence in Dharamsala. A party of eminent visitors filed past them and entered the building. It was another hot day, and the anticipation was hard to bear. Pema chattered excitedly, but Tenzin had stopped listening. In fact, he felt as if he might faint in the heat. Two hours passed before at last they were admitted inside.

Tenzin looked with apprehension at the crowd of officials standing before walls covered in *thangkas,* richly colored paintings of Buddhist deities. All the newcomers were arranged into rows, and told to sit on the carpeted floor. As he sat down, Tenzin recognized the Director of the Dharamsala Refugee Center, standing in the corner. He looked very thoughtful, maybe even nervous.

Everyone stood as the Dalai Lama entered the room. Next to Tenzin, Pema suddenly burst into tears and threw herself onto the floor in front of him. Officials rushed forward and pulled her to her feet. The disordered refugees were herded back into lines. Once again, officials signaled to them to sit on the floor. The Dalai Lama cleared his throat and welcomed the new arrivals from Tibet.

"You have come here to be free," he said. "We are living in exile as refugees, over 100,000 of us. You have come from the Holy Land of Snows. Remember that we are the owners of that land. We are essential to it. Although the Chinese oppress us, they cannot crush our people and our culture.

"Some of you have been given the opportunity to study here, so study hard," he urged. "And all of you must remember that this is not our country, this is India. If you want to stay here, even for a short time, you must work hard. And then— this is very important—you must return to Tibet."

The Dalai Lama paused to emphasize these last words, and looked around the room at each of the refugees. When he spoke again, it was slowly and deliberately.

"For without the people, the land will be lost and our culture will disappear forever."

The Dalai Lama's instruction seemed to make a deep impression on everyone, as silence descended on the room. But in Tenzin's mind, only one question burned: *Will I be allowed to stay with Pasang in India?*

When the speech ended, the refugees lined up to be presented individually to the Dalai Lama. He asked all the newcomers in turn what part of Tibet was their home and what plans they had for the future. He listened intently to each answer and offered a few words of advice. He blessed the refugees, placing a ceremonial scarf around their necks, and presented them each with a signed photograph.

Tsering shuffled forward to be presented, offering the bone of his mother for a blessing. The Dalai Lama cupped it in his hands and said a silent prayer over it. Tsering's cunning face softened with happiness. Pema was once again moved to tears in front of the leader, as was Dawa. Tenzin kept moving forward in line. Soon it would be his turn. This was the moment: his fate was about to be decided.

Tenzin stepped up and bowed his head. The Dalai Lama chucked him under the chin, raising Tenzin's eyes to meet his. Tenzin gazed up shyly into eyes that seemed filled with compassion and understanding. Pasang sprang forward to speak.

"I am his brother . . ." he started, then stopped short as the Dalai Lama turned and looked directly at him.

"Tell me, where is your home?"

Pasang's nerve deserted him. Awestruck, he stood speechless.

"How old are you?"

"Nineteen," Pasang stammered at last.

"Now study hard," the leader said crisply as he handed them both signed photographs. Pasang clasped his envelope and moved aside.

Suddenly he stopped short, as if realizing what had just happened. He had missed his chance to deliver the letter from the Director, or ask for a decision on Tenzin's future! Pasang whirled around, fumbling for the letter in his pocket.

At that instant the Director of the Refugee Center strode forward. He took the letter from Pasang's hand, and turned to the Dalai Lama. Bowing his head, he spoke rapidly about Tenzin's precarious position.

"The boy has no papers," he said, pointing at Tenzin. "At the moment, he has to go back home to Tibet." He called upon Pasang to confirm his words. Pasang nodded vigorously.

The Dalai Lama looked distressed. He turned to his officials.

"See to it that he is given appropriate papers. He must be allowed to stay in India to study. Make sure it happens," he ordered, his voice now severe.

Tenzin was still bewildered, and Pasang was too overwhelmed to speak. But His Holiness seemed to consider the matter concluded and was already talking to the next refugee.

As they filed out of the room, Pasang explained to Tenzin what this meant, hardly able to believe it himself: they would very soon be free to remain in India together.

"I am so happy," Pasang said simply, as they stepped outside into the sunshine. Everything around them seemed changed; friendly and full of possibilities.

"Now you have a choice," Pasang said. "You can go to school here, maybe to the Tibetan Children's Village, or come to the monastery with me. Do you want to be a monk or go to school?"

"I want to be a monk."

"Not school?"

"No, a monk."

"You want to be a monk? Why?"

"I don't want to be a student. I want to be a monk like you. With you, Pasang."

"Are you sure? It's not an easy life."

"Will you stay a monk, Pasang?"

"I don't know. Who knows what will happen in this life? But a monastery is a good place to be. You can study there, and learn Tibetan, and even English. You'll have food and a roof over your head. And I will be there to protect you and to make sure you are treated well."

"You won't run away this time?"

Pasang laughed, but seeing Tenzin's worried face, he said, "No, I won't run away. We'll be together."

Soon after, the Dalai Lama's sister invited the newcomers to the school. In a store stocked with second-hand clothes from western charities, she asked them to pick out replacements for their tattered jackets and trousers. Tenzin chose a red jacket, thinking of the red monk's robes he would soon be wearing.

Afterwards, Pasang told Pema that he and Tenzin would soon be leaving for the monastery.

"What will you and Dawa do now?" he asked.

"We're going to school!" she exclaimed. She and Dawa had decided to enroll at the school for older Tibetan students, known as the Transit School.

"It's down in the valley," she said excitedly. "Right now it's just a bunch of metal sheds. We'll study all day, and at night sleep in huge dormitories, in bunks stacked to the roof. I want to learn more Tibetan, and I hope English."

She thought for a moment. "Now that I've met the Dalai Lama I don't feel afraid at all," she added. "All the hardships we suffered, they weren't in vain. I'll stay here for two or three years before I go back to my home."

➤

The fugitives who'd come over the mountains together had been in Dharamsala for only a few days, and already many were moving on. Pasang and Tenzin gathered with them one last time at the bus stand in the town square, the very place where they had arrived. They talked for a while about their weeks in the mountains, and their hopes for the future. Sonam clasped Pasang's hand fervently as he said good-bye. For now he and Rinchen were embarking on a pilgrimage to Buddhist sites around India. They hoped to earn money as they traveled, taking odd jobs. And Tsering announced that he was returning to Lhasa.

"Easier to make a living begging there," he said. His leathery face cracked into a smile. "Here there's so much competition."

Pema and Dawa hugged Tenzin. The friends presented each other with *khatas*, the ceremonial white scarves that Tibetans give each other before a journey. The girls boarded the bus to the Transit School, waving as it pulled out. Soon only Pasang and Tenzin remained in the square.

Pasang touched the letter tucked in his pocket, as if to

make sure it was real. It was from the Office of the Dalai Lama, and it gave Tenzin permission to stay in India. The Director had sent a copy to the United Nations Refugee Agency. They were safe now.

Pasang and Tenzin picked up their bundles as another bus pulled in; this one would bring the brothers to the nearest railway station. Changing trains in Delhi and Mumbai, it would take them four days to reach Pasang's monastery in the Tibetan colony of Mundgod, in the southern state of Karnataka.

"If you think it's hot here, wait until you get to the south of India," Pasang told his brother. "But there's fresh drinking water in the monastery and plenty of showers, so you can always keep clean. The work will be hard, but we'll have regular meals, even meat on a Saturday."

Tenzin liked that idea.

Moments later, they boarded their bus. The band of travelers had broken apart, continuing their separate journeys.

➤

On his first day in the monastery, Tenzin woke at five o'clock in the morning, the usual hour for the monks to rise. His head was shaved, and he was given a novice's yellow-and-red robes to wear.

In the room he shared with his brother and two other novices, Tenzin sat on the floor, dunking a piece of unleavened *naan* bread into a bowl of milky tea. As he chewed, he thought about what would happen next. He was in for a strict regime and tough discipline, but Pasang would be there. His future seemed to be mapped out: he had a new country, a new home, a new vocation, and even a new name. As was the custom, his priest, the lama in the Drepung Monastery, had renamed him. From now on, he would be called Lobsang, "Holy One."

At the end of a bewildering day of new experiences, Tenzin returned to his room. There was something that he wanted to admit to Pasang, but he'd been unsure how to say it. Now that they were thousands of miles from home and their journey was over, the words at last came to him.

He waited until he and Pasang were alone. For a moment he watched his brother. Pasang had taught him so much, protected him through so many ordeals.

"Pasang," he began, "I'm happy here now. I'll stay here, study hard, and learn the Buddhist scripture." Tenzin paused. "But someday, Pasang, I want to go home. I want to see Mother again. And our brothers and my friends."

He watched for Pasang's reaction. His brother merely nodded.

Tenzin took a deep breath. "But I will never be able to tell them how difficult the journey was: how we had to steal food to live; how we were so cruelly treated by the guards; how when we crossed the Snow Mountains I got snow blindness and cried; how I missed Mother so much; how I could hardly walk because my feet were cut and swollen; how all the time I was so afraid of failing, of being sent back." The words spilled out now, everything he had been holding inside.

Tenzin wiped his eyes on his arm. Pasang was looking down, but Tenzin could see his cheeks were damp, too. Tenzin looked out through the monastery window to the world beyond. He knew that, for now, and for a long time to come, going home would be impossible.

"Pasang, will I ever see Mother again?"

"Of course," Pasang said quietly.

Tenzin reached under the neck of his novice's robe and found his mother's red blessing string. He had never lost it, and he never would. His fingers closed around the knot he had tied in the woods by the road; it was as secure as ever.

EPILOGUE

What Happened Next?

After a few months in the monastery, an unexpected letter arrived for the brothers. In great excitement, Tenzin hurried to the office to collect it. He thought that a letter had somehow reached them from home. But it wasn't from his mother. It had a stamp with a woman's head on it, and it came from England. He tore the envelope open, and with his new knowledge of English, and the help of another monk, he and Pasang read the letter.

It told them of a film that had recently been broadcast on British television, which showed Tenzin and Pasang on the Snow Mountains. A week or so later, a monk arrived from Dharamsala bringing a pirated video of the British documentary *Escape from Tibet*. It was screened in the monastery, and Tenzin was astonished to see himself and Pasang, and everyone else who had crossed the mountains with them, on the television.

Tenzin remembered the group of strangers they had passed in the mountains. But he'd never realized that he had been filmed; he hadn't known what a film camera looked like. The other novices were impressed, and for a time Pasang and Tenzin were minor celebrities in the monastery. More letters of support, money, and even bars of chocolate arrived from Europe, Australia, and the United States, from people who had seen the film. But for the brothers, studies and their daily schedule took precedence.

In the next few years, Pasang was ordained a Buddhist monk, while Tenzin went to school at the monastery and trained as a novice. During this time, they exchanged letters with several people around the world who had come to learn their story. And soon another door opened unexpectedly in their lives. A lecturer from King's College London offered them free tuition at their English Language School for two years, and generous sponsors agreed to pay for their passage from India. Pasang and Tenzin decided to grasp the opportunity for a new life.

On a cold November morning, they stepped off the airplane at Heathrow Airport in London. "The women here are so hardy," was Tenzin's first reaction. "It's too cold to be wearing such short skirts!"

After two years, they were granted the legal right to remain in the United Kingdom as Victims of Torture, and later they were given full British citizenship, which allowed them to return safely to Tibet when their brother Palden was married. It was a very emotional occasion when Tenzin and Pasang were reunited with their mother and brothers.

Today, Tenzin and Pasang have decided to make London

their home, and they are able to send money back to their family in Tibet. Both say that family is the most important element in their lives. Although they are no longer practicing Buddhist monks, they have kept their red robes.

The other refugees who made the journey over the Snow Mountains with them have had mixed fortunes. Sonam and Rinchen both achieved their ambitions to stay in India: Sonam joined a monastery, and his cousin took a job working in the fields in a nearby Tibetan colony. Tsering eventually made his way back to Tibet, where a few years ago he was seen successfully begging on the streets of Lhasa. Pema and Dawa spent two years at the Transit School in Dharamsala, learning English. Pema returned to Lhasa, where she worked as a guide for a holiday travel company. On one trip she met an American tourist who asked how she had learned to speak English. This woman was so impressed by the story of Pema's escape that she arranged for Pema to visit the United States, where she now lives. In Dharamsala, Dawa married a fellow Tibetan who successfully applied to study in London. When they flew to London, they became near neighbors to Pasang and Tenzin.

China and Tibet

Until the 1950s, Tibet was one of the world's least known places. Foreigners were actively discouraged from traveling there, and few westerners visited. But in earlier centuries, the country was one of the great powers of Asia. Tibetans competed with Mongols, Chinese, Manchurians, and Russians to establish great empires on the world's largest continent. Tibetan brothers Pasang and Tenzin are descended from Genghis Khan's Mongol horde, which swept across Asia in the thirteenth century.

Tibet has always had a turbulent relationship with its powerful neighbor, China. At times they have worked together; at times they have waged war. In 1949, the Communist leader Mao Zedong and his Red Army fought a destructive civil war in China, which ended in his victory over the Nationalists, the ruling party since 1928. Mao immediately proclaimed the foundation of the People's

Republic of China, and used a vague historic claim to justify invading the independent country of Tibet. At the time, Mao received the encouragement of Russia, as it was in the interests of both countries to counter Indian (and British) influence in Tibet. The Chinese people are taught that Tibet has always been part of the Chinese "Motherland," and supporters of the Dalai Lama are denounced as "splittist."

The occupation of Tibet offers great advantages to China, not only in providing space for its rapidly expanding population, but also because the country is the source of enormous quantities of exploitable resources. Tibet has water, timber, livestock, herbal medicines, and minerals. The mining of gold, copper, iron, coal, mica, and sulfite has become widespread, and oil fields are being developed in northern Tibet.

Today, the Tibetan government-in-exile based in Dharamsala, India, supports the Dalai Lama's longstanding policy of seeking autonomy, rather than independence, from China, with increased human rights for Tibet's people.

Buddhism and Tibet

Pasang was nine years old when he entered the monastery to train to become a Buddhist monk. In Tibet, boys and girls as young as five or six years old are placed in a monastery or nunnery. Although it guarantees them a good education, it is no easy life. They rise at five o'clock in the morning for two hours of meditation, followed by daylong teachings, debates, and prayers.

All Buddhists are taught early about the life of the founder of the religion, the Supreme Buddha, whose name means "Enlightened One." He was born a prince in northern India sometime in the sixth or fifth century BCE. Appalled at the suffering and cruelty in the world, he left his comfortable life to begin a pilgrimage in search of truth. His quest was fulfilled when he achieved "enlightenment"—the perfect peace of a mind that is free from ignorance, greed, hatred, and other harmful mental states— said to have occurred under a tree by the river Ganges. After that, he wanted to tell people the truth so that they, too, could use their own experiences to become free and enlightened.

Buddhist teachings include the beliefs that all living beings are equal in value, and that, despite the efforts of all people to find happiness, they must suffer pain. Buddhism offers freedom from such suffering through training in ethics, meditation, and insight. Buddhists believe in karma and rebirth, which means that all actions have consequences in future lives which continue until enlightenment is attained. Some beings achieve a higher level of enlightenment, and become Buddhas. Tibetans recognize the Dalai Lama as the reincarnation of the Buddha of Compassion, who has chosen to stay in this world to teach people the way to attain enlightenment.

Tibet: An Historical Timeline

1642 The Fifth Dalai Lama becomes the spiritual and political head of government in Tibet.

1645 Construction begins on the Potala Palace in the capital, Lhasa.

1935 The future Fourteenth Dalai Lama is born to farmers in a village in northeastern Tibet. Two years later, Buddhist officials declare that he is the reincarnation of the Thirteenth Dalai Lama.

1949 Communist leader Mao Zedong proclaims the founding of the People's Republic of China and announces the "liberation" of Tibet.

1950 China sends troops into Tibet. Over the next few years, Tibetan resentment of Chinese rule grows, leading to outbreaks of armed resistance.

1953 The first ascent of Mount Everest, the world's highest mountain, which straddles the Tibet–Nepal border, is achieved by New Zealander Edmund Hillary, with Tenzing Norgay, a Sherpa of Tibetan parentage.

1958 China initiates its Great Leap Forward program, a policy to reorganize its huge population of farmers and laborers. This results in widespread famine and starvation.

1959 A large-scale popular uprising breaks out in Lhasa. Chinese authorities suppress the revolt; thousands are reported dead. The Dalai Lama and most of his ministers escape over the Himalayas to India, followed by roughly 80,000 Tibetans. A Tibetan government-in-exile is set up in India.

1966 China's Cultural Revolution begins. In Tibet, many monasteries and cultural artifacts are destroyed.

1976 Chairman Mao Zedong dies. Successive Communist governments have continued the policy of repressing the Tibetan people. Large numbers of Han Chinese continue to be relocated to Tibet.

1989 China imposes martial law (rule by military authorities) on Tibet after riots break out.

1989 For his nonviolent campaign to end Chinese domination of Tibet, the Dalai Lama is awarded the Nobel Peace Prize.

2006 The Qinghai-Tibet railway, the world's highest, is completed between Golmud and Lhasa, linking Beijing to the Tibetan capital. The Chinese government hails it as a feat of engineering, as it is built over passes so high (5,000 meters/16,000 feet) that oxygen has to be pumped into the (Canadian-built) railcars. Critics say it will significantly increase Han Chinese traffic to Tibet, further undermining traditional Tibetan culture.

2008 The Olympic Games are held in Beijing. Months before the Games, protests in Tibet escalate into violence. Pro-Tibet activists in several countries disrupt the Olympic torch relay in an effort to direct world attention to conditions in Tibet.

A meeting of Tibetan exiles in India declares continued support for the Dalai Lama's goal of Tibetan autonomy, not independence, from China.

2011 The Dalai Lama announces his retirement from politics, but remains Tibet's spiritual leader. Exiled Tibetans elect Lobsang Sangay, a Harvard academic, to lead the government-in-exile.

2011 to 2013 Over 100 people are reported to have set themselves on fire in protest of Chinese rule in Tibet.

2013 China denies accusations that it has forced 2 million Tibetans to resettle in "socialist villages." It is now estimated that there are more Han Chinese than Tibetans in the country.

GLOSSARY

Cairn A pile of stones used to mark a boundary.

Chairman Mao Mao Zedong, leader of the Chinese Communist Party from 1935 until his death in 1976. His official title was "Chairman." During his leadership, in 1950, Chinese troops invaded Tibet.

Chomalongma The Tibetan name for Mount Everest, meaning "Mother Goddess of the World."

Chorten The Tibetan term for a Buddhist sacred domed monument used as a place of meditation.

Cultural Revolution Chairman Mao's campaign from 1966 to 1976 to reinforce Communism in China. He unleashed the Red Guards to stamp his authority on the country, including Tibet.

The Dalai Lama A Buddhist monk and Tibet's spiritual leader, his title means "Ocean of Wisdom." Tibetans revere him as the Reincarnation of the Living Buddha of Compassion. From 1642 until recently, successive Dalai Lamas have led Tibet's government.

Dhal bhat Nepalese staple dish of rice and lentils.

Dharamsala Town in India where the Dalai Lama and many Tibetan refugees have settled.

Diviner A monk with supernatural insight into the future.

Drog-pa Nomads of Tibet.

Electric baton A battery-operated prod used as a torture instrument by Chinese police. It causes pain by inflicting a high-voltage, low-current shock.

Great Leap Forward Chairman Mao's disastrous policy to reorganize China's labor and agriculture. It resulted in widespread famine and starvation throughout China and Tibet. It is estimated that out of a population of 6 million, 1 million Tibetans died during this time.

Han Chinese The majority ethnic group in China.

Karma The positive outcome that Buddhists believe is produced by good deeds, affecting a person's future lives.

Khata Sacred white scarf, given to those about to set out on a journey.

Lama In Tibet, a Buddhist spiritual leader.

Mani stones Special slates carved with Buddhist prayers.

"Namaste" Traditional greeting in Nepal and India.

Prayer flags Colored cloth rectangles printed with prayers, often strung in high places such as mountains, where the wind may carry their blessings through the region.

Red Guards Units of zealous troops created by China's Chairman Mao to combat opposition to the Cultural Revolution.

Refugee status Official recognition that a person is outside their country in order to escape war, persecution, or natural disaster. Countries that have agreed to the United Nations' Convention Relating to the Status of Refugees must respect the rights of refugees who seek safety in their territory.

Reincarnation The rebirth of the soul in a new body. Buddhists believe that a person can be reincarnated many thousands of times.

Rupee Indian currency.

Snow Mountains The Himalayan mountain range, which includes the highest mountains in the world.

Stupa The Sanskrit (ancient Indian language) term for a Buddhist sacred domed monument (see **Chorten** on page 151).

Tsampa Toasted barley, a Tibetan staple.

Tuberculosis (TB) A bacterial infection of the lungs, to which Tibetans are susceptible.

United Nations Refugee Agency The organization founded after World War II to oversee global refugee issues.

Yuan Chinese currency, worth about 10 cents each.

ACKNOWLEDGMENTS

Foremost, I want to thank Pasang and Tenzin for telling me their story, and also for the gift of their friendship.

Several people gave me both advice and encouragement in writing this book—especially my wife, Ann, and her goddaughter Lizzie Spratt. I also want to thank the crew from Yorkshire Television who worked with me on the documentary and became Pasang and Tenzin's first friends from the West: Mike Shrimpton, Hugo Smith, Chris Barker, Mark Smeaton, and Francisca van Holthoon. I am especially grateful to His Holiness the Dalai Lama for writing a foreword.

The first edition of *Escape from Tibet* was self-published in Britain in March 2012; its modest print run sold out within a few months. Subsequently, Annick Press asked Laura Scandiffio to work with me on a new edition of the book. I want to thank Laura for her complete understanding of the story, and for expressing it so well in this new edition.

Nick Gray